The CAKCHIQUEL ALBUM

THE CAKCHIQUEL ALBUM

Edited by Ethel E. Wallis

W. F. Jordan, R. R. Gregory,
W. Cameron Townsend

GIFT PUBLICATIONS
Costa Mesa, California

*Bible references are taken from
the King James Version*

*International Standard Book Number: 0-86595-006-7
Library of Congress Catalog Card Number: 81-81502
Gift Publications, Costa Mesa, CA 92626*

*Design: Pete Berg
Back cover photo: John B. McIntosh*

Contents

Foreword

Twenty centuries of Christianity have produced a small, elite class of God-servers whose names have also made secular history. Wycliffe, Luther, Calvin, and Carey—such men have occasionally changed the course of human history.

Wycliffe, "the morning star of the Reformation," dared to make God's Word audible in the crude cadence of his earthy mother tongue in fourteenth-century England. Until his day, sacred revelation was the possession only of the privileged clerical class. His efforts were rewarded by fanatical persecution, but Wycliffe's Bible changed the shape of sacred and secular history, making an irreversible impact on English life and letters.

Four centuries later William Carey, nurtured on the Scriptures in his mother tongue, left England for India where, as "the father of modern missions," he translated the Bible into Bengali for millions who had never heard the name of Christ. Through prayer and pains he travailed to bring to birth a team of translators who gave the Scriptures to four major languages of India. His academic achievements also laid the foundation for India's educational system.

Both Wycliffe and Carey translated for major languages; Wycliffe, for his own native English, destined to become a vehicle in world communication; and Carey, for Indian languages. Carey created a dynamic model for modern missions by leaving his homeland, learning unwritten tongues, and translating the Bible. Following his example, pioneers translated in 700 languages in Asia, Africa, and the islands of the Pacific by 1900.

In the tradition of Wycliffe and Carey, William Cameron Townsend pioneered in a language of Latin America, completing his task in 1931. In May, 1981, Wycliffe Bible Translators celebrate the Golden Jubilee of the publication of the Guatemalan Cakchiquel New Testament, the "firstfruits" of Townsend, their founder. Cakchiquel was a minority language, spoken by 250,000 pre-Colombian Indians geographically and linguistically isolated by the prestigious Spanish tongue surrounding them. Townsend's translation changed the course of Cakchiquel history, but few outside of Guatemala would feel its impact.

But history may yet assign Townsend a significant role, not for the Cakchiquel translation per se, but for the movement which it initiated. As early as 1920, when the dynamic Bible expositor L.L. Legters participated in the first Cakchiquel Bible conference, sharing with Townsend information of Bibleless tribes in the jungles of South America, the vision of translating the Word for *all the minority languages of the world* began to emerge in the minds of the founders of Wycliffe Bible Translators. Neither Wycliffe nor Carey could have dreamed of a task of such staggering proportions. It could have come only to men of the twentieth century, men like Townsend and Legters.

When Cameron Townsend went to Guatemala in 1917 to sell Spanish Bibles he fully intended to return to California to complete his college course. But his higher education was to be consummated on the Cakchiquel Indian campus where he learned to speak an unwritten language, devise for it an alphabet, translate the New Testament, and teach the Cakchiquels to read it. He established schools and a hospital; he encouraged Cakchiquels to form 100 of their own congregations. This pioneer achievement provided a working model for the Summer Institute of Linguistics and the Wycliffe Bible Translators, founded by Townsend and Legters to reach the ethnic groups of the world with the written Word.

The pattern set in a work of God in the formative years often casts predictive outlines of the future, if the original model warrants reproduction. The growth of WBT-SIL speaks for itself: in 1981, 4,000 team members at work in some 800 minority languages around the world, around the clock, devising alphabets for them and translating the Bible.

Cameron Townsend in 1981 completes eighty-five years of life, sixty-four of which have been spent in sharing the blessings of the Christian heritage with groups of over-looked people deprived of this privilege. This small volume provides a glimpse into the first segment of his long and productive life, with a brief picturesque panorama of the formative period preceding the formation of WBT-SIL. The original form and features of the photographic and verbal reports of the 1917-1931 chapter of Townsend's life have been preserved. The photos are untouched, the words in their original eloquence. The first two sections were written by American Bible Society men personally involved in the Cakchiquel translation. W. A. Jordan traveled with Townsend over rugged rural Guatemala trails, sharing the humble hospitality Indian hosts provided. R. R. Gregory attended the dedication of the published New Testament in 1931. His eye-witness account captures the live excitement of the historic occasion.

The story of Antonio Bac, written by Townsend, reveals the unfeigned esteem in which he held his uneducated Indian colleagues. A sense of equal partnership and mutual concern is faithfully reflected in Townsend's appreciative account of the work of an intelligent, innovative Cakchiquel leader. And Townsend's constant concern shines through the words revealing his thought patterns in the 1920s as he labored alongside his beloved Cakchiquel brethren.

His words and phrases may have been modified for the 1980s but Townsend's challenge is unchanged: God's Word in the mother tongue of every ethnic entity on planet earth demands the highest priority among mission objectives. Without an understandable Word, no group of people however large or small can join the song long sung by the missionized majority: "The church's one foundation is Jesus Christ the Lord."

How can they believe in Him of whom they have not heard—or read?

Ethel E. Wallis
Linguist/Translator
Wycliffe Bible Translators, Inc.
Huntington Beach, California
February, 1981

I

William Cameron Townsend: Pioneer Missionary to the Cakchiquels

W. F. Jordan
Secretary, Upper Andes Agency
American Bible Society

From CENTRAL AMERICAN INDIANS AND THE BIBLE

Fleming H. Revell Co., 1926, pp. 13-44

William Cameron Townsend: Pioneer Missionary to the Cakchiquels

How it thrills one to meet the pioneer, the man who not only has had visions and dreamed dreams, but who has had sufficient faith in the visions and the dreams to dedicate his life to bringing them to pass. Such a man is William Cameron Townsend, formerly of California, now of Panajachel, Guatemala. We first learned of him in 1917, when, as a colporteur, he was itinerating Central America on foot accompanied by an Indian carrier, and subsisting on a mere pittance of twenty-five dollars a month. Since then we have followed his career as he has blazed the trail among the Cakchiquel Indians of Guatemala. Recently I have been permitted to meet and travel with him, visiting group after group of Indian Christians ingathered largely as a result of his ministry.

Having decided to become a missionary, William Townsend left college at the close of his junior year. He wished to acquire some practical experience before proceeding further with his studies. A year on his chosen field, he thought, would give him a better idea of just what he most needed in order to complete his missionary preparation. His college course remains incomplete. He has not yet found a stopping-place in his missionary activities.

The first twenty months in Central America were spent in the work of distributing testaments, gospels, and tracts. Three times during this period Mr. Townsend made the journey on foot from Guatemala City to El Salvador, the capital of the neighboring republic, each time taking a different route. On these trips he met, conversed with, and preached to all classes, from the humblest Indian peon to governors of provinces. He also made a journey on muleback through Honduras and Nicaragua. He carried no food supplies but always subsisted on corn cakes and black beans secured from the natives and slept wherever night overtook him, whether in the country home of the wealthy planter, on the porch of the one-roomed shack of the peon, or in the vermin-infested hut of the Indian.

As a result of the experiences acquired on his Bible-distributing trips Mr. Townsend knows the whole country as few others. After studying the situation and considering the subject from every angle, he came to the conclusion that from a missionary viewpoint the Indians were the key to the situation in Guatemala. They constitute two-thirds of the population and have a physique, a stability of character, and a persistence not possessed by those of Spanish blood. Aside from the work done by Dr. Paul Burgess of the Presbyterian Mission among the Quiche of Quezaltenango, little organized effort had been made to reach them. Missionary endeavor had heretofore been chiefly directed to evangelizing the *ladino*, as the mixed race of that country is called.

The Cakchiquels constitute some 200,000 of the 1,250,000 Indians in Guatemala. At the time of the Spanish conquest they were the most warlike of the Central American tribes and offered the greatest resistance to the Spaniards. They had made remarkable progress in civilization. Part of their religion consisted in the worship of the maize plant, and it is thought that they were the people who first redeemed it from its wild state and reduced it to cultivation. The world, therefore, probably owes these Indians a greater debt than it can ever repay.

After their conquest in 1542, the Cakchiquels, along with other Indians of Guatemala, were exploited with merciless cruelty. Las Casas avers in his history that between four and five million perished as a result of the cruel and barbarous treatment to which they were subjected. In spite of laws placed from time to time on the statute books, ostensibly intended for his protection, the Indian of Guatemala is still looked upon as the personal property of the landlord, considered a beast of burden, and occupies a position a little better than that of slavery. He is transferred with the land that belonged to his forefathers—is practically bought and sold. Not an uncommon advertisement in the newspapers of Guatemala is—

FOR SALE—
Plantation with its Indians.
Owner going to Europe.

One of these Cakchiquel Indians had accompanied Mr. Townsend on his evangelistic and Bible-selling trips, and this man's mental and spiritual progress, as soon as he was treated as a man instead of a beast of burden, had demonstrated the possibilities of the Indian character and had inspired the young missionary with a great desire to take them the Gospel. His own denomination having no work in the section occupied by the Cakchiquels, Mr. Townsend applied to the Central American Mission which already had a few small congregations of Indian believers. Mr. A.E. Bishop, the superintendent of the Mission, had long been looking for a man adapted to this particular work, and Mr. Townsend's application was accepted. Entire charge of the work among these Indians has since been given him.

Soon after his appointment to the Indian work of the Central American Mission, Mr. Townsend was married to Miss E. Malmstrom of the Presbyterian Mission of Guatemala City. The ladino town of Antigua, the old Spanish capital, was first chosen as headquarters because of its being the administrative and market center for a large and densely-populated Indian section. The Townsends soon found, however, that so long as they lived among the ladinos it would be impossible for them to get into sympathetic contact with the Indians. They were so far removed from them, socially, that they seemed to be made of different clay and to be living in a different world. Mr. and Mrs. Townsend decided on heroic measures. Five miles away was the large Indian town of San Antonio Aguas Calientes. Here was a congregation of Indian believers and here lived Silverio Lopez, the successful Indian evangelist. They would establish their home in San Antonio. Here they would be right among the people they were trying to reach and still not too far from the center of the District.

But, how to secure a house? No one in the Indian village was willing to rent or sell to a white man. Finally, without waiting for the action of the Mission Board, Mr. Townsend seized the opportunity to buy a small piece of land and began to build on it a most simple little house with sides and partitions of cornstalks, roof of secondhand tiling, a rough board floor, and no ceiling. The cost of this humble home when completed was but seventy dollars, which amount was donated by the native congregation of Guatemala City.

With great curiosity and interest, the Indians watched the progress of the work on the building that was to house their missionary. Seeing the uprights that Mr. Townsend placed at different points in the interior of the framework, they were puzzled and ridiculed them. They said that these posts would not serve any purpose and would only be in the way. When he came, however, to put in the partitions attached to these uprights, they saw the purpose of them. Strange to say, the Indians even approved of the idea of separate rooms. Although they had never before had any in their own houses, they themselves are now beginning to separate with light partitions the interior of their own one-roomed barnlike shacks, a first step to a higher plane of living. Four hundred years of contact with his European oppressors had not made the Indian wish to adopt the custom of living in a partitioned house. A single house built in his midst by one who loved him made him wish to live in one like it.

Soon after the Townsends moved to San Antonio, prejudice against them began to break down. Their untiring attendance on the sick during epidemics of influenza and malaria convinced the Indian that the missionaries were his true friends. Before long more land was secured, and through the help of a boyhood Sunday school teacher who had learned of the work of her former pupil, more substantial buildings were erected. The Mission property now consists of a small chapel, a day-school building, a house for the missionary in charge, a home for the fifty boarding pupils from surrounding Indian villages, and a hospital building. The same building that houses the boarding pupils serves as a home for the lady missionaries who have joined the Townsends in the work.

While Mr. and Mrs. Townsend no longer live in their first cornstalk home, this is still in service, being occupied by a worker and some boy students. As I visited this primitive dwelling and realized the self-effacement necessary to make happy in it red-blooded Americans who had been accustomed to physical comfort, I did not wonder that success had attended the efforts of this young couple. They had willingly spent two years of patient waiting for better things while occupied with the tremendous task of acquiring an unwritten language, learning the psychology of a strange people and the meaning of peculiar customs, as well as winning the friendship of a suspicious non-Christian community.

The Cakchiquel work has grown beyond all expectations. Twenty Indian converts have expressed their desire to become preachers. These enthusiastic students meet every other month at the school for Indians in Panajachel to study under missionary teachers the things that will help them to become more efficient in their work. The alternate months are spent in preaching and evangelizing.

The large number of Cakchiquel converts has made increasingly important the translation of the Gospel into their tongue. The Mission Board has recently released Mr. Townsend from all other duties until the translation of the New Testament shall be completed. Besides this volume, which will be published by the American Bible Society, he is also at work on a manuscript grammar and dictionary of the Cakchiquel language, a pioneer enterprise of greatest importance in the task of "teaching all nations." It is the work of such pioneers that has given the world the "Good News" in more than 700 languages and dialects. May their numbers increase until all of the many doors opening throughout Central and South America shall have been entered and none of the numerous Indian tribes can say, "We have never heard," for each one shall have welcomed its pioneer apostle.

A Scrap of Paper Starts
Things in Guatemala

Dejected and discouraged, a Cakchiquel Indian was making his way home to Santa Catarina, Guatemala. He was returning from a visit to the witch doctor. The cause of his dejection was the illness of one of his children, following the recent death of another after a long period of similar suffering. He was discouraged because, in spite of all his efforts and faithful following of the directions of the witch doctor, the child continued to decline.

The witch doctor had assured Silverio, the Indian father, that the sickness was caused by the unrest of the spirits of his forefathers, who had taken up their abode in the abdomen of the child, causing the abnormal swelling. In order to pacify these restless spirits the father must burn candles before the nearest volcano, under sacred trees, and within the chapel of the local saint at Antigua. In the case of the first child, the candle-burnings had all proved useless, and the stricken father had no reason to hope that they would be more effective in saving the life of the little one who was now suffering.

Silverio was dissatisfied with the witch doctor. When the first child had been taken sick the man had promised relief if his directions were faithfully followed. Now he promised relief again, but he had given the same prescription. However, there was no alternative; Silverio must follow the directions of the witch doctor, because he alone was supposed to know causes hidden from common people. Therefore, more candles must be burned, more pilgrimages made to prescribed shrines, and more money paid out from the father's scanty earnings with no assurance whatever in his own mind that any good would come of it all. Meanwhile his beloved child was suffering and growing weaker day by day—modern medical science for the Indian of Latin America is nonexistent.

As Silverio proceeded sadly on his journey his downcast eyes caught sight of a fluttering piece of paper. Curiosity prompted him to pick it up and he began laboriously to spell out the printed words. In his boyhood he had learned his letters but had never profited much from the acquired knowledge, and the Spanish in which the words and sentences were printed on the paper was still a foreign language to him.

The scrap of paper was a leaf of one of the gospels containing the account of Jesus turning the mercenaries out of the Temple. The words used by our Lord on that occasion stuck like a barbed arrow in Silverio's memory: "It is written, my house shall be called a house of prayer, but ye have made it a den of thieves." The statement seemed to have an apt application to the subject of his thoughts. The witch doctors who professed to be his spiritual leaders had repeatedly taken his money and given him nothing in return. They were thieves indeed. The sentiment expressed fitted his present mood exactly.

Showing a friend the torn leaf, he was told that it was a part of the Bible. Years before Silverio had purchased a

Bible from a traveling colporteur, but he had never been able to get any satisfaction from reading it because of his deficiency in the knowledge of Spanish. He had therefore put the Book away and had almost forgotten that he owned a Bible. The curiosity aroused by the scrap of paper prompted him to dig up again, from the bottom of the box where it was stored, this Book which contained the statement that had made such an impression upon his mind.

Silverio knew that the Protestants believed the Bible contained a message from God. He decided what to do. He would take the treasured Book to Isidro Alarcon, the nearest Protestant pastor, who lived four miles away in Antigua, the ancient capital of Guatemala. He would ask him to explain its meaning.

In Mr. Alarcon the poor Indian found a sympathetic friend. The faithful pastor not only explained the meaning of the text in question, but also preached Christ to his visitor, and told Silverio so earnestly of His love that he not only believed and received comfort in his own soul but enlisted at once in the service of his newly-found Master. Learning of the child's illness and mistrusting the cause, Mr. Alarcon gave a simple remedy that soon disposed of the parasites that were causing the trouble attributed by the witch doctor to the spirits of his ancestors.

Immediately on his return home, Silverio began to preach Jesus to his fellow-townsmen in the twin Indian municipalities of Santa Catarina and San Antonio. Such a complete change was there in his life and so effectively did he testify to the power of Christ to save, that within one month forty men and women were converted. This little group of new converts sent in an earnest appeal to the Central American Mission for a pastor to be located among

them. Thus began the Indian work of that mission in Guatemala. At the time of the writer's visit, Silverio Lopez was
pastor of five Indian congregations. A fifteen-year-old son,
who accompanies him and plays the folding organ that he
carries with him on his itineraries, is also preparing to
devote his life to the work of teaching. Great things for Silverio Lopez, his family and his people, date from the
thoughtful perusal of that fragmentary message.

The Indian town of San Antonio has become the center
of a large and rapidly growing work. The number of Indian
believers has increased in a short time to more than 2,000.
In the attempt to meet the need of the Cakchiquel Indians
and enter the open door for their evangelization, there have
been established an orphanage and boarding school for children of the converts, and a hospital with several beds, in
charge of a nurse who holds a daily clinic and ministers to
such sufferers as come for treatment. A modest chapel and
a home for the missionaries have also been built. A school
for the training of native Indian evangelists has been established at Panajachel, an Indian town in sight of beautiful
Lake Atitlan. Two Indian translators, working under missionary direction and supported by the American Bible Society,
are busy at the task of translating the New Testament into
their own tongue, thereby adding another to the many languages in which the printed Word is being circulated. The
gospel of John, made on a mimeograph, has appeared as
the first book ever published in Cakchiquel. The other gospels together with the Book of Acts are already in manuscript and undergoing final revision before publication in
book form.

Power of the Memorized
Bible Verse

We were drawing near Cajahualten, the end of the first stage of our muleback journey from San Antonio to Panajachel, Guatemala, and I listened eagerly to the story of the beginning of the work in this place, where we were about to spend the night.

Five years before during an evangelistic tour, Mr. Townsend and Mr. Treichler found themselves on an unknown trail in this mountain gorge. They were evidently quite lost. It was late in the afternoon and night would soon overtake them. There was no danger, but the thought of spending the night on the cold mountainside without shelter, and with nothing but the single blanket each carried to keep out the piercing chill, was anything but pleasant. Fortunately they met a man who proved to be an Indian convert. He told them of a nearby hamlet of which they had never heard. The people there, he said, were very much interested in the "Good News." Thankful that their immediate needs would be met, and that they would at least find food and shelter, the weary travelers gladly accepted the offer of the Indian to guide them to the place.

On their arrival at the group of huts the missionaries met with a cordial welcome. Their hearts were cheered by the glad hospitality offered, though it consisted of but the coarsest fare and an opportunity to sleep on the bare floor of one of the primitive one-roomed dwellings. When they announced their willingness to hold a service, word was sent out into the neighborhood and a congregation of eager listeners gathered, and the joy of preaching the Gospel to a group who had never before heard a missionary was theirs. The testimony of the converted Indian had, however, been seed sown in good ground and the harvest was ready for reaping. Fourteen Indians, then and there, took the first public step in the Christian life.

One of those who made their first public confession the night of the missionaries' visit was Cixto Guajan. Some time previously Cixto had intended celebrating the festival of his saint. In Guatemala, as in many other countries, it is customary to name children after some saint in the Roman calendar. The image or picture of the saint, after being duly baptized by the nearest priest in return for an adequate fee, is set up in the home and becomes the protecting deity of the individual bearing its name. Instead of celebrating their own birthdays each year, they celebrate the festival of the image. The Indian believes that he honors his idol by getting drunk on the day of its festival; the idol is grieved if he does not get very drunk. A poor Cakchiquel Indian woman, crawling along the road, was urged to go home and sober up.

"I am doing this for the Virgin Mary," she said, indignant that she should be thought to be getting drunk and disgracing herself for her own pleasure.

Cixto was on his way to see if he could borrow the money he needed for this drunken celebration when he met the same Christian Indian who guided our lost missionaries to the hamlet. The man preached the Gospel to Cixto and told him that God was not pleased with drunkenness. The message that stuck in Cixto's heart and memory was the statement that God was everywhere, and that he, ignorant as he was, could pray to Him in his own home, in the field, anywhere. Cixto was so impressed by this simple message that he returned home without attempting to borrow the money with which to get drunk. Going away by himself, he got on his knees to pray and remained there until comfort came to his soul. He then began to talk to his brother-in-law, an older man, about his new faith. The brother-in-law became very angry.

"So the cursed evangelists are after you?" he said. "I will kill them if they come to my house."

Both Cixto and his brother-in-law were among those converted at that first Christian service in Cajahualten.

Poor Cixto was ignorant, inexperienced, and unlettered. His former friends united in persecuting him and in assuring him that he had been deceived by the foreigners. He began to wonder if, after all, he had done right. One day while hoeing in his little beanpatch on the mountainside, he decided to settle the matter by prayer.

"O Lord," he cried, "if the Gospel is not true, show me; and if it is true, make it plain to me so that I can explain it to others."

At the next preaching he received the answer to his prayer. He caught, understood, and memorized his first Bible verse: "For God so loved the world, that he gave his only begotten Son, that whosoever believeth in him should not perish, but have everlasting life."

The next day, as his only answer to his persecutors' jibes, Cixto repeated this verse. He improved with every opportunity to attend a preaching service, and each time learned some new Bible verse. During the interval between services, he would evangelize his fellow-Indians with the verses learned. He became a very effective worker and the rest of his career was characterized by his readiness to quote Scripture texts and his skill in applying them. In eighteen months he had learned to read and had married a Christian girl who was able to play a folding organ. Cixto and his young wife then toured the country together on foot as colporteur evangelists, he carrying the folding organ on his back from place to place. After two years of this work, the Lord took him home. His young widow continued in the work, and is now helping in the mission hospital in San Antonio.

As my companion, Mr. Townsend, finished the story we were met by some Indians with the news that the old trail had been destroyed by a landslide and that they had come to show us the way around. So rough was this new trail that we were obliged to dismount and lead our mules.

Arriving at the chapel just before dark, we found awaiting us a group of twenty-four Christian Indians. The grass-thatched building in which the service was held belonged to our host, Jose Chate. The hero of "The Scrap of Paper," and pastor of this as well as four other growing congregations, was my interpreter. His son was there with the baby organ. The humble room was lighted by rude, homemade, beeswax candles suspended from the rafter by means of strings and bent wires. Under these circumstances I addressed my first Indian congregation in Guatemala, assured that the more abundant entrance of the Word would bring increased light, both physical and spiritual.

When the congregation had dispersed we placed the

benches together for a bed, and Mr. Townsend spread on the seats the cornstalks that we were to feed the mules in the morning. While these were not particularly soft, they served to break the unyielding monotony of the boards. Spreading over the cornstalks our ponchos and blankets, we retired to pass the night of visions of spiritual opportunities—although not of physical comfort. In the morning, after partaking of some beans, coffee, tortillas, and honey provided by our host, we set out on the road to Comalapa, a large Indian town that was opened to the gospel message by the humble Cixto Guajan, whose memorized texts were so signally blessed to himself and others.

Some Cakchiquel Centers and Outstanding Converts

Comalapa is the largest purely Indian City in Guatemala. We approached the town just before nightfall, and the groups of women coming from the public fountain with water pots on their heads gave it a closer resemblance to the large villages of British India than any other place I have seen in the Western World.

A PAGAN CITY

Until the arrival of the Bible colporteur, Comalapa was wholly idolatrous. In this town the primitive Indian custom of stealing the wife still prevails. A young Indian, having decided that he would like a certain girl for his home, confides this to a male friend, and the two lie in wait for her as she passes along the road in company with some older woman or companions engaged in carrying water or in some other service. The young men rush unexpectedly upon the girl and, if too much resistance is not made by her companions, drag and carry her off bodily to the home of the suitor. Then follows a series of palavers between the father of the young man and the parents of the girl. Generally an agreement is arrived at by which the father of the girl receives a certain sum of money and relinquishes the daughter. Sometimes, however, they fail to agree. In such a case the father of the boy pays damages for the outrage, and the girl returns to her parents.

The idolatry of the Indians of Comalapa is not that of the philosopher who reveres the image because of the superior being represented in it. No, the image worshiped by the Guatemalan Indian, however grotesque, ugly, or mutilated it may be, is the very god itself. Their witch doctors are of two kinds, significantly called in their own language the "Priests of the Sun" and the "Priests of the Devil." And as their names would lead one to believe, the Priests of the Sun are less vicious than those of the devil. The practice of the former consists largely in divining the causes of sickness and giving advice as to which images, volcanoes, trees, or stones must be appeased by burning candles and incense in order to obtain relief. The Priests of the Devil are called upon to exorcise evil spirits and are supposed to have the power to bewitch their enemies. These Priests of the Devil are much feared.

As we went through the town Mr. Townsend pointed out that idol shrines abounded in Comalapa as in no other town he had seen. These shrines are little houses situated on the street. They frequently occupy a corner lot and are filled with images before which candles are kept burning. But their evil influence is beginning to wane before the light shed by the Book, even though up to the present the message has come in a strange tongue. How much greater things may we expect when the message of love reaches them in familiar language of the home.

In Comalapa is spoken the purest Cakchiquel dialect; that is, with the least admixture of Spanish words. For this reason the language of this city is being taken as the standard for the Bible translation work now under way. Before final correction, the manuscript is being read to intelligent groups of Indians in Comalapa in order to make sure that no words or expressions have crept into it that will prevent the message from being understood by isolated groups of Indians who have not come in contact with Spanish civilization.

A LONG WAIT

Ventura Otzoy, of Comalapa, purchased his first Bible from a colporteur twenty years ago. He could not read, but bought the Bible out of curiosity because of the Spanish name "Santa Biblia," and because he was told that it was God's Book. For fourteen years the Book remained in his home unread, but he and his sister were constantly on the lookout for someone who could help explain it to them. One day, hearing that an evangelist colporteur, the faithful Cixto Guajan, had passed through the town, the sister pursued and overtook him, and asked him to come to their house and read and explain the Book to them. This Cixto did, remaining as guest with Senor and Senora Otzoy for a week, during which time Don Ventura and his family, together with a married brother and family—ten persons in all—accepted Christ as their Saviour and destroyed their idols. Though fifty-five years of age and a confirmed drunkard, Don Ventura at once abandoned the use of intoxicating liquors.

So grateful was Don Ventura for what the Lord had done for himself and family, that he built, with the help of his son, and dedicated to the work of the Gospel the prettiest chapel that I saw on my way through Guatemala.

Here in this substantial building, erected and dedicated to
the Lord by a Cakchiquel Indian converted as a result of
Bible colportage work, my message was interpreted by
Felix Chicol, the local pastor.

FROM DRUNKARD TO PREACHER

Felix Chicol was the son of a well-to-do Indian of Comalapa. His father had not only trained him in carpentry and
the simple tailoring required in an Indian town, but insisted
that he learn to read for the prestige it would give him.
Young Felix was quite popular. He was induced to join one
of the idolatrous secret organizations, and was made secretary. This introduced him in an official capacity to all the
religious festivals of the city—debauches, they might better
be called—and he became an incorrigible drunkard.

After drinking up all the property inherited from his
father, Felix borrowed money from the agent of a coast
planter and obligated himself to work as a peon on the
plantation until the debt was paid off. Ordinarily this
would have been the last of Felix. With his habits, he had
practically sold himself into life servitude. His appetite
would call for more drink and keep him under a debt.
Physically, socially, and spiritually he was a lost man. One
day, however, he heard the Gospel and was converted. He
immediately changed his living habits. Not only did he give
up drink, but beginning at five o'clock in the morning he
put in long hours at work, in order the more quickly to pay
off his debt. As soon as he was free, Felix returned to tell
the story of Jesus to his old companions in sin and vice. He
reached Comalapa at the time of the dedication service of
the new chapel just completed by Otzoy. His testimony

and appeal to his old friends will long be remembered.

"You all know me," he said, "I am Felix Chicol. My father left me lands and education. You made me secretary of your religious organization and I became a drunkard. I went in with you with money, good clothing, in my right mind, decent, and came out a hog. That is what your religion did for me. Now I have come to Christ and His saving grace. He has changed me and I have come to tell you all about it."

Felix developed fast, and soon began to devote all of his time to preaching and evangelizing. He is now pastor of the home church in Comalapa which is steadily growing under his leadership.

TESTED BY PERSECUTION

Comalapa produced one of the first helpers in the work of translation of the gospels into the Cakchiquel language, Margarito Otzoy. Don Margarito's father was well to do for an Indian and his uncle was one of the chiefs of the city. They were of the same clan as was Don Ventura, the converted carpenter. Margarito was an intelligent boy and because of his father's position in the community was able to get some schooling.

Margarito's first knowledge of the Gospel came through hearing Cixto Guajan's earnest preaching on a street corner from some of his memorized Bible texts. He followed him to the house where the indoor service was afterwards held. The simple message gripped his young heart and he was truly converted.

The early converts in Comalapa suffered much persecution from their fellow-townsmen and Margarito's sincerity was immediately put to the test. His own father drove him from home and disowned him. The uncle, who was a chief, was one of the principal persecutors, not only of his nephew, but of the mission church in general. He incited a mob to throw stones into the congregation and to fire shots through the door of the chapel in his efforts to break up the meetings. He made false accusations against several of the converts and had them imprisoned and kept them at hard labor for six weeks, during which time they were dependent upon friends for all the food they received and to gather the evidence that enabled them to prove their innocence of the crime with which they were charged.

Margarito proved faithful through it all. The fires of persecution but brightened and helped to establish his faith. He had assisted Mr. Townsend with the translation of the gospel of John, and our business in Comalapa was to arrange if possible for the employment of all of his time in translation work until the New Testament should be completed.

Although our business in town was with Margarito, we could not leave without holding a service in the chapel built by Don Ventura. While I was speaking, two Indians, whose dress and bearing indicated their importance in the community, entered the chapel, saluted cordially the native pastor and Mr. Townsend, took their seats and listened attentively throughout the remainder of the service. With the little congregation that has passed through the fire we rejoiced at this evidence that blind prejudice is breaking down before patient, consistent, Christian living of the small group of converts in Comalapa.

A MIXED CONGREGATION

Early in the day, after leaving Comalapa, we descended for some two or three thousand feet the side of a precipitous gorge, along the bottom of which flows a stream that furnishes motive power for a grist mill. Some little distance from the mill we found a congregation of fifty persons gathered at the home of a believer. This was the only mixed congregation of Indians and ladinos that I saw in the Cakchiquel country. Here Spanish was more or less understood by all, the services of an interpreter were not needed, and Indian, ladino and foreigner united in worshiping one common Father and in listening to the message from the Book He has given us.

This flourishing church had one of those humbling origins which I have found to be an interesting and encouraging feature of the work in Central America. An itinerant colporteur evangelist sold a Bible to a man who was unable to read. The man loaned the book to his brother who lived in this canyon off the main throughfare. The brother read and studied the Book and talked to his wife and children and neighbors about it, and the effect was such that when the next itinerant evangelist called at his house the whole family believed the Good News. They immediately turned their home into a place of worship, and today a congregation of Indian and ladino believers gathers there to hear the preaching of the Word.

II

The Cakchiquels Receive the New Testament in Their Own Tongue

R.R. Gregory
Secretary, Caribbean Agency
American Bible Society

Panajachel, Guatemala
June 15, 1931

The Cakchiquels Receive the New Testament in Their Own Tongue

The Indians of Guatemala are coming into their own. For the first time in the history of these folks has the entire New Testament been translated and published in one of their dialects. A few years ago the evangelical work among these people was a negligible factor. Today the situation has changed. The account of present-day mission effort in Guatemala must reckon with the ever-expanding work among the aborigines of the country.

Twelve years in this rapidly moving age is a long time to wait to see one's dreams realized. It must have been a never-to-be-forgotten day to Mr. and Mrs. W. C. Townsend when at last they saw the complete New Testament in Cakchiquel presented to a representative group of Cakchiquel believers at a special conference held at Patzum May 19 and 20.

Two pictures representing two groups of Indians shall ever have a place in my memory. During the feast days at Patzum, a decidedly Indian town of about 5,000 population, these two groups had their eyes turned toward the same town. The one group was large in numbers. Many of them had saved for months in order to enjoy themselves in the celebration of their patron saint's day, San Bernardino.

Each day the procession with two images of San Bernardino proceeded from the Roman Catholic church. No doubt that saint would have smiled to see two images of himself—one to satisfy the ladino element and the other the Cakchiquels—paraded through the streets.

The main street was lined several blocks with booths. The plaza in front of the Catholic church was likewise filled with tables and stalls where all sorts of wares were for sale to the Indian population that was expected to gather from points miles around. It was a beautiful sight to see the Indian women dressed in bright colors, strings of colored beads hanging around their necks; the children dressed up for the occasion; little babies strapped to their mothers' backs and in a contented mood looking around. The men, too, in their peculiar, tribal dress attracted our attention. Here and there from buildings came the sound of touching marimba music, also that of the guitar, violin and other instruments. Crowds gathered on the outside looking in and beholding groups making merry over wine and song. These places of iniquity and debauchery with their liquor, music and revelry were the chief attraction for many. At evening time, one might have seen, several miles before entering Patzum, a continual stream of Indian men and women returning to their grass-thatched homes, many of them staggering, moaning and letting out weird cries, victims of a commercialized traffic in human weakness bent on making the celebration of a Roman Catholic saint a success.

The second picture was made up of a group of Indians by all odds smaller. Mr. Townsend, Trinidad Bac and I were late in arriving at the conference, having been detained the day before at Guatemala City where we had an appointment with the president of the republic, in order to present him the first copy of the New Testament in Cakchiquel. On the morning of the twentieth our auto stopped at the edge of town, within an enclosure beside the little chapel where the conference was in session. At last the hour arrived when the Cakchiquel New Testament was to be formally presented to the Cakchiquel brethren.

Mr. Carl Malmstrom, head of the Robinson Bible Institute, was in charge of the program. Mrs. Malmstrom and Mrs. Townsend were seated each one at a folding organ—and how the congregation entered into the spirit of the song service! Spanish and Cakchiquel hymns were sung. "Showers of Blessing" was a favorite one. Prayers by various workers were full of thanksgiving and spiritual fervor. There was special vocal music by Mrs. Townsend and her nephew. The Caribbean Agency Secretary of the American Bible Society was called upon for the opening address, and to make the presentation of the Cakchiquel New Testament. The theme selected was taken from II Chronicles 34:15—"Finding the Book." The speaker told of how the lost Book was given to the King, an interpreter of the Book brought it to the King, the people of Judah assembled and the Book was read to them; and the resultant revival. The hope was expressed that the Cakchiquel New Testament might find its place likewise among the 200,000 Cakchiquels.

The first copy of the New Testament had been presented to the president of the republic the day before, and now the second copy was turned over to a fitting representative of the Cakchiquels—some have called him the Paul of his people. Trinidad Bac has an understanding of the Scriptures and a facility of interpretation that is most remarkable. He is easily the spokesman of his people. He was one of the two native translators who accompanied Mr. and

Mrs. Townsend to the States where after a year of intense
work the Cakchiquel New Testament was finally gotten
ready for the publishers.

It was a happy moment for Trinidad Bac as he received
the New Testament from the representative of the American Bible Society in the name of his people. All eyes were
turned toward him for half an hour as they listened to him
express in Cakchiquel his own joy in having a book that
gave the story of the life and death of Christ and the history
of the early Church and the precious writings left by the
other writers, in the dialect of his own people.

He rejoiced in the fine workmanship put into the Book.
Bound in one of the colors of his national flag, printed in
clear type and with excellent quality of paper, the Book
appeals to the artistic sense of the Indians, and Trinidad
spoke of the fact that God's Word was honored by appear-
ing in beautiful form. He added that he hoped that this
Book would mark a new day in the life of his people and
give impetus to a revival as took place and was recorded in
Chronicles.

Then followed a season of prayer. What pent-up emo-
tions were let loose and what heartfelt gratitude to God was
expressed; what joy filled the hearts of the expectant congregation! Yes, we all were of one mind that "it was good
to have been there."

There were other presentations made that day. The third
copy was presented to one who, although absent, will receive the copy in due time. It was given to Mrs. C. H.
Greenleaf, who for a number of years has shown unusual
interest in the uplift of the Cakchiquels. For several years
Mrs. Greenleaf has contributed liberally and has made
possible the continuance of the Bible Institute at Panajachel,

an Institute exclusively for training Indian workers to carry the Book and its message to the Indians of Guatemala. Twenty-three young men are at present attending that institution. Four copies were also presented to young men who had rendered valuable service in translation work. What a splendid group of workers!

In spite of a shower during the afternooon service, the enthusiasm of the congregation was not dampened as special song and praise continued. The representative of the American Bible Society spoke on "The Unfinished Task of the Church." However, the climax of that meeting was reached when Mr. Townsend was called upon to tell the story of "The Hand of God in Translating the New Testament into Cakchiquel." Mr. and Mrs. Townsend are dearly beloved by the brethren.

It was inspiring to listen to Mr. Townsend as he opened his heart and spoke of difficulties within the camp and without; how he had made a vow that the work would be completed, and how in the midst of it at times it seemed almost impossible to continue; how broken health several times threatened to block the way of advance; how the only solution to the problem was to move to the States and take loyal natives with him and finish the work there. And then, during those early years, the difficulty in attempting such a work without a grammar and a dictionary to depend upon; and then, too, the profound spiritual truths to be expressed in a language which seemed so poverty-stricken in words to convey such thoughts. What a triumph of faith and patience!

Mr. Townsend paid warm tribute to his colaborers and to the courtesies and invaluable suggestions given by the general secretary of the American Bible Society. Selected portions were read from the Cakchiquel version. Many of the women who understand very little Spanish but speak almost exclusively their own tongue, bent forward as they listened, while the expression on their faces gave proof that they understood.

The evening session marked the close of the conference. The rains broke in upon us anew and at many places water dropped upon the listening congregation. Messages were given in both Spanish and Cakchiquel. The brethren were not in a hurry to close the evening service. The chairman asked for a final word from the Bible Society representative, but before that could be given a Cakchiquel worker begged for permission to speak just five minutes. Measured by the enthusiasm of the brethren, great things are to be expected in the days to come.

Finally, I was asked to give a final word. This was very short: a request that verses 24 and 25 of Jude be read from the Cakchiquel version as a closing benediction of the conference.

Just another paragraph given in a reminiscent mood: I shall never forget the eleven-day trip on muleback accompanying Mr. Townsend in visiting a section of the Cakchiquel field some six years ago. One day as we were climbing a long mountain slope, we talked about many things. I remember Mr. Townsend as he related an incident that took place in his student days and left an abiding impression on his life. The preacher spoke to the student body from Psalm 78:41 on "Limiting God." From that day on, Mr. Townsend decided that he was going to let God have a chance at his life.

God has wrought a mighty work through this humble servant. The story of giving the New Testament to the

Cakchiquel Indians is but a part of his services. There are scores who through his personal ministry have been brought to a miraculous change of a new life. He is still dreaming dreams. The last few days I have listened to him as he has hinted at some of the big problems yet to be met—the great needs of the backward Indian tribes of Guatemala and all the untouched millions of Indians in South America. The great masses of Indians cannot read and write. The next few months an intensive campaign is to be carried on whereby groups of workers are to meet with Cakchiquel brethren in strategic centers to prepare them to teach others to read. Oh, the need for Christian schools among these people!

The other day, Mr. Townsend said to me, "One thing I cannot understand. During my deputation work in the States, I noticed that money could be secured to endow schools that were already a duplication of effort, but down here where the need is so great, it is so difficult to secure sufficient funds for the uplift of a people that have been neglected for centuries." I know that the burden of his heart is that, through prayer, young men and women rich in intellectual and soul life, and men and women of means, will refuse to limit God in their lives and will give Him a chance in carrying out a great task where the doors of opportunity are ever opening wider.

III

Cakchiquel Evangelist Antonio Bac

W. Cameron Townsend
Founder, Wycliffe Bible Translators

Unpublished manuscript

Guatemala, 1930

A Burden and a Book

The Christ-given work of the Church is to preach the Gospel to every creature. Sad to say, however, she has been too easily tied up with other things, from politics and social service to bitter theological wrangles. The urgent command of her Lord has been neglected, and now after twenty centuries the real work of the Church is still far from finished. Oh, that she would understand! Oh, that she might have the mind of her Master! That her eyes might be closed to all else and opened to her duty! That she like Paul might realize her awful debt (Rom. 1:15), "strive to preach the Gospel," and say, "This one thing I do." How quickly would her task be done and her Lord brought back to right the wrongs which she can but feebly help!

On the mission fields where the Gospel has but recently arrived there is the earnest desire on the part of almost every believer to pass the Good News on to all those who have not yet heard. A convert's first thought is to tell the other fellow of his new-found Saviour. Many believers leave all and give their whole time to preaching the Gospel to the regions beyond. God works miracles through these modern apostles.

Among the Indians of Guatemala, one of the most

remarkable of these preach-the-Gospel-to-every-creature men is Antonio Bac, and it is in the belief that many more privileged Christians in the homeland will be inspired by this uneducated but valiant soldier of the cross that this story of his life is written.

Antonio's father was a drunkard. This is nothing startling. It is a custom, in fact a religious obligation, to drink. The saints in heaven, argues the Indian, would be dishonored did not their namesakes on earth make merry on their special feast days by getting drunk.

Mothers put rum on the tongues of their nursing babies to get them "accustomed," they say. In some towns, the father or witch doctor anoints a youth with liquor in consecrating him to some idol. Primitive marriage vows are made over a bottle of rum. In cases of sickness, liquor is the most trusted remedy, even for horses. One of the most ridiculous sights the writer ever saw was a horse made drunk by rum poured down his throat to cure him of the colic. Rum is far more common than bread in Indian homes. A town without a bakery, a meat market, or a drygoods store may have several saloons.

Antonio's father drank a little more than others. He was a Quiche Indian but had wandered away from his people and settled among the Cakchiquels in Patzum. The mother of his children (75 percent or more of Indian couples live together without being legally married) was a Cakchiquel so that Antonio learned the latter dialect. Their home was a thatched hut where the cold of the 7,000-foot altitude was kept out by canes plastered over with mud. Mother never sat on so much as a stool, much less a chair, but squatted on a mat on the hard mud floor and would grind the corn into batter on a large stone, pat it into pancake-like tortillas, and bake it over a fire made between three stones on the ground. The same mud floor served as table and bed. Clothes were ragged and thin, for wages were poor and father was a drunkard, and mother too. Nevertheless, Antonio had a taste of home life as a boy until his father went off on a trip and probably got drunk and died, for he never returned. Then there was nothing for mother to do but to become a servant in a Spanish-speaking home.

Thus it was that Antonio grew up running errands for those who looked upon him as just an Indian, a beast of burden, whose utility would be ruined should he learn to read. Consequently, Antonio never went to school, though he did learn Spanish fairly well. This is more than most Indians accomplish, the great majority being able to speak only their own dialect. Those who are said to be able to speak Spanish can merely bargain and carry on other simple conversations, while deeper thoughts expressed in Spanish are understood by very, very few.

Like most Indians, Antonio married very young. He became a drunkard like his father. An Indian who drinks generally has to borrow money. In fact, he often borrows from the saloonkeeper, usually a representative of some plantation on the lowlands. He then has to serve a certain length of time on the plantation with part of his wages going to the saloonkeeper as a reward for having entrapped him in the meshes of the forced-labor system. Antonio became thus obliged to take his family once a year down to the unhealthy climate of the lowlands to work on a plantation. Deep in poverty he sank, even deeper into sin.

Now an Indian in sin is just like any other human. He seeks relief in some kind of worship. He indeed has various religious facilities. The *aj-kij* or "Priest of the Sun" calls him to worship the forces of nature or even the spirit of some tree or hill.

The old nature worship has more to do with the crops. The worship of the spirits of trees and hills is resorted to in cases of sickness. The witch doctor is also appealed to. But the great resort when the sin question is faced is the pilgrimage. Many an Indian has become tired of his sins and has gone on a long pilgrimage to some famous shrine to seek relief.

This is what Antonio decided to do when the weight of sin kept growing heavier and heavier. He decided to seek help from the so-called "god of Central America," the "Black Christ of Esquipulas." This is an image of Christ on the cross which is supposed to have fallen from heaven in early days following the Spanish conquest. The sculptor made it black so as to attract more the attention of the Indians. A large temple has been built for it in the town of Esquipulas and thousands journey to it from all over Central America every year. For Antonio, it was a trip of more than two weeks. He had to carry on his back all his food, and candles as well to burn before the image. Up certain grades he had to carry stones to do penance, which he would deposit at the foot of the cross on the summit and then sweep off his sins with twigs. Before other crosses he had to dance. Upon reaching the shrine, he approached it on his knees and pled with the black image to free him from his sins. Then he went sadly out and lo, the same old appetite within forced him into a saloon to drink. He was still a slave.

Before spending all his money, however, he bought a miniature image of the black Christ to take home. He would become a devotee of the god and erect an altar in his own home. Thus it was that he returned home the proud possessor of an image of the black Christ. His boss greeted him on his return and congratulated him on the prize he had bought. He asked him if he had noticed whether the image was of wood or wax, saying that one had to be careful "nowadays," for many deceivers were abroad selling wax images which were apt to melt when one burned candles near them. Antonio's heart sank within him. Could it be that his god was of wax? He was afraid to make the test and duly set up the altar for his image, but with less faith in it.

After some time, two of Antonio's children became sick. His immediate desire was to burn candles before his black Christ. When all his candles had been burned up he sent his eldest daughter to buy more, saying at the same time that if the image didn't hear his prayer and heal the children he would burn it. The girl became frightened and said, "Papa, you'll suffer for disrespecting our saint."

All was in vain and one of the children died. Friends were called in for the funeral and liquor, of course, flowed freely. Antonio, quite tipsy by that time, recalled his threat and rose up saying, "I'm going to burn that mean black saint." The neighbors, however, were horrified and all cried out against him, preventing him by force; and so the impotent image remained in its place as the family god.

One day a Bible colporteur passed through Patzum and sold a Bible to Antonio's boss. His wife and neighbors, however, objected to the Book, so he decided to sell it, offering it to Antonio for the same price he paid for it. It was a large, beautiful book, and Antonio had become ambitious to learn to read, so he bought the Bible. With a few lessons from friends and much pondering over his Bible by the light of a pine torch, he learned to read. He liked everything he read, as did his wife and family.

Then a revolution broke out and Antonio was taken to serve in the army. The Bible was left on the altar before the black Christ.

One day a report came to his wife that Antonio had been killed. Much troubled, she decided to take refuge with her mother. She gathered together what she and the children could carry and started to leave their home. Then she remembered the Bible and, though it weighed four pounds and she already had a heavy load, she put it into her basket. She started off with the heavy burden on her head, a baby on her back, and an ache in her heart. But God had so worked that the treasure which she wanted to save was the Bible while she was willing to leave the black image to the fate that might befall it. Her mother scolded her for this, and wanted her to burn the Book, but she would not. The report of Antonio's death was false and later when he returned to his home he found the black god had been stolen to grace the altar of some other Indian hut.

Reunited, the Bacs decided to leave Patzum and move to a lowland plantation where the war with poverty could be waged with greater success. Once settled in their new home, the question arose, "What shall be our family god now that the black Christ is gone?" All voted in favor of the big Bible, and it was duly given the place of prominence upon the altar and incense was regularly burned before it. Like Moses' brazen serpent of old, the treasured but little-understood volume had become an idol in their eyes.

Upon a visit to the capital, Antonio procured a book from which he professed to learn the meaning of dreams and could read the future. Being gifted with an unusually bright mind, he became accepted as a witch doctor. This opened up another source of revenue, but the folks whom he deceived too often brought their pay in the form of rum and Antonio became a drunkard. All the vices encroached upon him, and rapidly he sank deeper and deeper into sin. His robust body began to break under the strain of debauchery, and Antonio came face to face with the fear of death.

From Suicide to Life Eternal

Then a strange thing happened in Antonio's old home town. Luis Lonus, an Indian of Santiago, perhaps the first Cakchiquel believer, came to Patzum for a visit. As an Indian evangelist he had been laboring for many months to reach his people with the Gospel. It seemed to be in vain. Missionaries had been working for more than thirty years among the Spanish-speaking race and thousands of converts attested to their faithfulness and the power of their message. But none of them had been able to learn an Indian language, all being too busy with their Spanish work. They saw the need, however, for the patient, dark-skinned burden-bearers were before them every day and on every hand.

In the markets, missionaries purchased their fruit and vegetables from Indian toilers of the soil who had carried their heavy loads of produce for many miles under the burning sun. Wood and charcoal came from the same source. The roads were full of Indians all burdened; men and women and children all carried their loads; but as they returned from the market with empty sacks and baskets they touched Christian hearts of pity still more, for there was in greater evidence the more awful load of sin. The restless cried out for drink, and did not seek in vain. Liquor was cheap and sold on every hand. Every road, even in the most out-of-the-way places, had its saloon where the Indians left much of the meager proceeds of their labor. Many a drunken Indian, toppled by the wayside, would meet the missionary's pitying gaze. Children were often seen trying to awaken their mother or father from a drunken stupor to take them home. More drink would be poured down the father's throat to stimulate him for the remainder of the journey. A whole group made tipsy by the "fire-water" would frequently be seen engaging in a brawl. The Indian problem was appalling.

The descendents of the original possessors of the land still constitute 60 percent of the population. Deep in poverty, ignorance and sin, they were completely subservient to the ruling Spanish-speaking class, which treated them as dogs. But what could the missionaries do? The Indians were separated from them by differences in blood, language, dress, social standing, customs, and modes of thinking. Clearly they constituted a special problem and needed special missionaries who would learn their languages and adapt themselves to the problem. But none could do it, and as the last resort the missionaries made special efforts to evangelize those Indians who understood Spanish. The converts would then be used as evangelists to their own people. The system was far from perfect, for it did not permit much growth or development in the Indian work, but it was the best that could be done under the circumstances, and Lucas Lomas was the first of those emergency workers among the Cakchiquels.

God uses any instrument surrendered into His hands. He uses many an untaught emergency worker on the mission field far more than many highly-trained workers in the homeland who have not fully surrendered themselves to Him. A fine working principle for any servant of God is to find a place of need which no one else is willing to fill and then to tell the Lord, "Here am I. You have no one else to use here at the moment. You must use me, incapable though I am." God loves to use "the weak things of the world to confound the things that are mighty" whenever and wherever these "weak things" are surrendered in His hands.

Lucas had a pointed wit and a winning way. It is said that upon a certain occasion Lucas went to a gypsy camp to give out tracts. A fortuneteller grabbed him by the arm and pulled him toward the tent door saying, "Come! Let me tell your fortune." The old man resisted but in vain, until his quick wit came to aid his feeble body. "Wait," he said, "let me tell your fortune first." The gypsy halted in surprise with, "What, you tell my fortune?" "Yes," replied Lucas. "If you don't believe on the Lord Jesus Christ and quit this wicked business, you'll go straight to hell."

With his own people, his manner of approach was extremely gentle and also dignified. He was received as a prophet, a special messenger from God, and as such he was always welcome wherever minds had not been prejudiced against him beforehand. The writer accompanied him on a house-to-house canvass in Santa Maria Jesus. The Gospel was new to the Indians and they listened with reverence. Nearly a dozen times that day we were invited in to have a cup of coffee or eat a bite of food. In a district where the Gospel has never been preached, the worker is often received as a saint. The Indian as he listens to the message of God's love will fold his hands and look toward heaven, saying, *Matiosh chiri Dios! Matiosh chiri Dios!* ("Thanks be to God! Thanks be to God!") Some urge one to partake of their food. Others offer gifts of money. The writer has even had incense burned before him. Many kneel and want to kiss the hands and feet of the one whom God has sent to tell the message.

But Satan sows his seed. These simple folk, at first so eager to hear, are told that we are deceivers. Our words are admitted to sound beautiful at first but the warning is that later we talk against all that is good and even against God.

It is generally believed that we have horns and are in league with the devil and that when a person receives a treat from us, we become owners of his spirit and forthwith take it to a hole in a nearby volcano where the devil appears and catches the soul on his pronged fork when we throw it to him. Then he sends bags of money to us with which we subsidize those who profess the Gospel. Believers are said to have horses' faces. When they die it is believed we put their faces downward in the coffin, evidently to facilitate a downward journey into hell. Such tales are legion and result in making the timid Indian fearful of the Gospel. One who believes immediately becomes an outcast from his people. He is no longer a person. He may even be put in jail or his house burned, though the government does its best to prevent such abuses on the part of the local authorities.

If such is the persecution today, how much more must Lucas Lomas have suffered as a first Cakchiquel believer. He had been bitterly tried. Once he and a companion were driven out of a town by a mob. Taunts awaited him on every side but he continued, "despised and rejected" as his Lord, but with a meager knowledge of the Scriptures due to the fact that they were not in his own language. Nor could any missionary explain their meaning in his own Cakchiquel. Poor and advanced in years, this faithful soldier of the cross continued, and praise God that he did!

Patzum was some thirty miles away from Lucas' home town. There he was little known. So it was that with a light heart one memorable day he began his house-to-house canvass in the Indian section of town, for there he would be respected and his message heard with unprejudiced ears. God led Lucas that day just as He led His apostles of old. He led him to the home of Miguel Ajpop (*Miguel mat-maker*). Miguel was a dour old man, so highly esteemed in the eyes of his people that his home had been selected to be the official image deposit for that section of the town. He was reverenced and held a place of authority among the Indians. All Miguel's money went to keep candles burning before the images whose steward he was, and in providing for bombs and skyrockets as well as "firewater" to make hilarious the birthday of the patron saint. On this festive occasion, the old man sat with a happy smile stroking his patriarchal beard, rare among the Indians, and watched the young men make merry, some dressed up like deer turning somersaults on the thatched roof. Others were drinking and dancing alternately, until the drink he himself had imbibed would gain the victory over his senses and he would topple off his stool before the image.

Lucas found the old man sober and in an amiable mood. He had invited Lucas into the image room and sat there with his little wife Michaela while Lucas expounded to them the Scriptures. *Matiosh chiri Dios! Matiosh chiri Dios!* was their cry of appreciation as they raised heavenward their gnarled hands in worship. Lucas was invited to return and this he did on frequent occasions. Finally he was permitted to hold a service in the image room. He had invited a few other interested Indians to attend. Several professed to accept Christ, including old Miguel.

Services were continued in the same spacious room. Nothing was said of the images. Christ's work on the cross and His power over sin in the life of a believer were proclaimed. One day, however, when Lucas came, the image was gone. Miguel had made it known that he no longer believed in his wooden gods and would give them away to anyone who came for them. They went as fast as remnants on a bargain counter, and when Lucas came the room had been cleared and converted into a chapel.

One of the first believers was Trinidad Bac, Antonio's younger brother. Fear arose in Trinidad's heart, for Antonio was a bad man and it was dangerous among Indians for a man to try to teach his older brother. But he had learned to pray and as he prayed for his brother, God's Spirit worked. Antonio became extremely despondent and told his wife that he felt as though he were going to die. The only relief that he could get was from reading his Bible which he did with frequency. For two months while Trinidad prayed, Antonio felt more and more power of the Holy Spirit's convicting work.

Then Trinidad arrived. It was a walk of fifteen miles over a mountain and through a forest from Patzum to Chikaquish where Antonio lived. Trinidad's heart was fearful, but he had read of Andrew in the Bible who first found his own brother Simon. Trinidad determined to do likewise. He had prepared the ground with two months of intercession, then introduced his message with a prayer fifteen miles long. Oh, how those believers pray! An Indian evangelist compares it to the oil used in a machine. He says he cannot work without it. As he journeys along he must go aside into the bush to commune with his Master and seek His blessing upon his work.

Antonio received his brother in a "wiser-than-thou" attitude. He had had the Bible for twenty-one years and felt that he knew more about it than his younger brother. It was Trinidad's first effort at evangelizing and soon it seemed that Antonio had entangled him with arguments. Trinidad's last resort was to a hymn—the first hymn he had learned—and Antonio followed the words as his brother droned out in Indian chant, "I will sing the wondrous story of the Christ who died for me." As Trinidad earnestly and prayerfully dragged through the three verses, these words began to take hold of his brother's heart: "the Christ who died for me." His conscience was awakened. He saw his sins as a black cloud and at the same time all that he had read in the Bible flashed through his mind with new meaning. That hymn saved the day. Antonio promised to think the matter over and even attend a Gospel service in Patzum.

This he did, but the Indian who gave the message that day was unwise in his manner of approach and antagonized Antonio so that he refused to go again. Still Trinidad continued to pray, and the force of conviction became stronger in his brother's life. Antonio became haunted by his sins. They appeared blacker and blacker before him. Finally he became desperate. He decided to end it all by death.

His wife and children he sent off to Patzum. When all alone, he took down his old muzzle-loader and filled it with powder and shot. As he prepared to pull the trigger, he felt a strong presence which said, "Quit." He obeyed and the voice continued, "You must ask permission of the Heavenly Father before you do that awful deed." He felt another influence which said, "Go ahead—why delay?" But Antonio obeyed the voice which called him to prayer.

He took his Bible and went out into the forest. Alone there with only the two presences struggling for influence over him, he knelt down and said, "O Father God, what dost Thou want me to do?" The evil presence seemed to flee. The presence of Christ became more real, and directed him to open the Book. Accustomed to his book of necromancy in his witchcraft, he now opened the Bible expecting to find an answer to his prayer. He did not look in vain. His finger fell upon the place telling how Judas hanged himself, and of how it would have been better had he never been born.

Then he opened it a second time and Romans 8:1 met his glance: "There is therefore now no condemnation to them which are in Christ Jesus." The voice came clearly once more: "You are pardoned." He felt the assurance of eternal life, and rose from his knees as a new Antonio Bac.

School in the Forest

The miracle of conversion is the great proof of the Gospel. There is no greater testimony in the eyes of the world than that of a transformed life. Marvelous indeed are the conversions which daily occur upon the mission field. Doubters are puzzled and scoffers silenced by the power of the Gospel to save from sin the most degraded who believe. An atheistic plantation owner once reproved the writer for giving his time to the "foolishness of preaching." The owner was asked if he had never had the occasion to see the effect of the Gospel among his laborers. He was frank enough to admit, "Yes, I have. I don't understand it, but it is a fact that these who accept are regenerated."

Another landowner told how, two years before, he had purchased a large plantation in the district of Zecapa. Much of the land was covered with jungle but he determined to bring it under cultivation. A trip was made to the plantation. What was his surprise upon arriving to find that the laborers had practically taken possession of the property. Being far away from towns, in a wild lawless section, they had become law unto themselves. They lived, planted, and harvested on the owner's land but refused to help him with his work. Nor would they provide him food to eat; and he, finding himself in such a predicament with even his life imperiled, abandoned his property.

A year later with fear and trembling he determined to make another visit to his land. A cordial welcome awaited him. The same laborers who had refused him food before now served him a chicken dinner. In a body they presented themselves before him, asked forgiveness for the way they had treated him, and gladly offered to work for him in the future. He could not understand what had changed them from semisavages to perfect gentlemen. Then the spokesman explained: "We are Christians now, sir. A few months ago God sent a preacher of the Gospel here. He taught from the Bible all that Christ did for us and we accepted Jesus as our Saviour. We have surrendered our lives to Him and would serve you, too. The only request we would make is that you give us liberty to worship God as we believe." Gladdened beyond measure, the owner replied that not only was full liberty theirs but he would also give them the manor house for their services while he would build himself another. Many of his friends and relatives also have become convinced of the truth of the Gospel through this incident.

No wonder that many unbelieving landowners call our workers to preach the Gospel to their laborers! The believer no longer drinks or engages in brawls. He is a faithful and more intelligent workman. His honesty can be depended upon. The change wrought in his own home is wonderful. As a byproduct of salvation comes a train of material blessings. Debts are paid off first of all, making the Indian a free man. Then dirty, tattered rags are exchanged for respectable clothes. Homes are improved; beds are installed and bedrooms moved out of the kitchen; chairs and tables are purchased and the grinding stone is put upon a stand. Even a writing desk is found in Antonio Bac's home. It is a crude but ingenious arrangement. Two wooden boxes have been nailed together and legs attached. The boxes are on their sides and within each is a smaller box which serves as a drawer. Over the top an Indian shawl has been neatly spread as a table cover.

And then another change is brought to pass in the believer. Antonio had lost his health before believing, but even that was restored to him. The whole family profits. When drinking and superstition have gone, health and happiness enter the door. Among unbelievers the infant death rate is sadly high. Among converts it is not so bad. Children receive opportunities never dreamed of before their parents accepted Christ.

Our Indian schools provide Christian education and a healthy environment to many little tots who would otherwise grow up in ignorance like their fathers. A little more than a year ago, Antonio and his wife took two of their boys from the mountain home and left them at San Antonio to go to school. What a wonderful day it was for those children! They are learning not only to read and write, but other elementary studies as well as the Scriptures. Can we not hope that those boys will turn out to be stalwart Christians?

But all these changes were far from Antonio's mind when the glorious light of the Gospel burst upon his soul. There upon his knees in the forest he received the gift of eternal life.

He then and there covenanted with God to return that life a living sacrifice to the Giver. His happiness knew no bounds. Back to the hut he went and unloaded the gun.

Then he tore down his images and threw them into a ra-
vine. His next thought was to make known what Christ
had done for him. With Bible in hand he proceeded to the
plantation and there told all of his old friends that he was
now a believer in the Gospel. He was the first convert on
the plantation and his boldness shocked everyone. They
told him that the devil had deceived him, but he disproved
it from the Scriptures. Then they tried to intimidate him by
saying that in the capital all believers were being killed. But
they didn't know Antonio Bac. The information only fired
him. His life was no longer his own, and he would gladly
lay it down for his brethren. He returned to his hut, rolled
up his blanket and threw it over his back, hid his long knife
under it, and started on the sixty-mile walk for the capital.

He went directly to the penitentiary but could see no one
being slaughtered. Puzzled, he hunted out the home of a
man he knew to be a believer. The Christian rejoiced to
know of Antonio's conversion but laughed when told the
object of his visit. "Come with me," he said, "I will show
you how much truth there is in what they have told you."
He took a bunch of tracts, gave some to Antonio, and took
him out into the street to give him his first experience at
tract distribution. Even the policeman received the printed
message politely. No one molested them. Then followed a
simple study in the Word, after which Antonio started
home.

His life on the plantation was not an easy one. Many
were the persecutions. Especially when the laborers were
drinking was he heavily beset with trials. Many would become greatly offended when he refused to drink with them.
Among the Indians it is considered an insult not to take a
glass with a friend. In one town a number of believers were

thrown into jail and fined because they refused to drink with the town mayor. A young believer named Luis Sagche (*Louis White-tree*) was once returning home from market in Antigua when an old friend greeted him from a road-house and invited him to help in emptying a bottle of rum. Luis meekly replied that he no longer drank and begged his friend to excuse him. The friend took it as an insult and struck him with his machete. Luis dodged the blow, seized the man around the waist and threw him to the ground.

Then he held him while he explained the reason he no longer cared for the "fire-water." He made plain the love of God and the way of the cross until the drunkard's eyes filled with tears and he pled for forgiveness. Another believer refused a proffered glass, whereupon the contents were spitefully thrown in his face.

The Gospel is the great enemy of drink. The collector of revenue in Antigua made the statement that the consumption of liquor had decreased 25 percent in San Antonio since the Gospel entered that town. Not only do the believers quit drinking but their influence also has a good effect on others. Once a believer in San Antonio named Julian was stabbed by a drunken man. It was before the days of our own hospital, so he had to be carried on a stretcher four and a half miles to the government hospital in Antigua, run by Catholic nuns. He died before treatment could be given. The next morning a friendly saloonkeeper asked our schoolteacher if it was certain that the wounded man had died. When the reply was in the affirmative, the liquor seller exclaimed, "Poor man!" An Indian standing in the doorway, a bottle of liquor in his hand, broke into the conversation: "Don't call Julian a 'poor man.' He is happy in heaven now while I with my bottle am going to hell."

There is an idea prevalent among the unbelievers that we cure converts of drunkenness by some remedy or magic. Many drunkards will seek us out and beg us for a remedy. What a joy it is to point them to Him who alone is the remedy and can make them free if they will but believe in Him.

Once an Indian from Santiago Zamorra came with his wife to seek the cure for drunkenness. They brought a gift of a basket of vegetables, much as though they were seeking a consultation with the witch doctor. The man's story was pitiable beyond description. He was a slave to drink but a slave who longed to be free. He told of his ineffectual efforts to shake off the shackles. He had recently consulted his father-in-law, who was something of a seer. The old man listened to his son-in-law tell of how he would call and call upon God for relief but to no avail. The grey head shook in an all-wise way. "You have done foolishly, my son," came the reply. "You should pray to the devil. He is the one who has power over the vice of drink." The man acted upon the advice but with poor results, for Beelzebub was not disposed to loosen his grip.

At last the drunkard had braved the "magic spells" of the missionaries and had come to seek relief. The way of salvation was prayerfully explained. The man was urged to accept Christ, but it was no use. He was like Simon the sorcerer—his eye was on the gain. His farm yielded him unusually good returns but drink kept him poor. In order to become rich he wanted to stop drinking, but there was no repentance-working faith in his heart.

Antonio Bac was not such a man. He had been a terrible drunkard but Christ had saved him. He now hated liquor with a righteous hatred and when urged to drink would refuse, saying, "No, I wouldn't even take that stuff for medicine."

John the Baptist and the apostle Paul learned theology in the wilderness. Antonio Bac got his start in the forest. There by the light of a pine torch he would ponder over the Scriptures. Soon he became convinced that his book of necromancy was a stumbling block to him. Immediately he threw it into the fire. Then he felt he should witness, and straightway he was about it. He heard, however, that the lives of believers were often threatened by fanatical hearers. By way of precaution he would keep his dagger handy beneath his shirt. But God graciously prevented him from using it until he came upon the verse which says, "They that take the sword shall perish by the sword." At once he decided the issue. He would carry the dagger no longer.

And so it was that alone in the forest Antonio Bac grew in the knowledge of the Scriptures in preparation for a great work. His arguments were always based on Bible verses. They were always timely and accompanied by exact citations. The writer was once at the point of going surety for a believer who was in debt. Antonio at once spoke up and asked if he had never read Prov. 17:18. A believer was once complaining to Antonio over the loss of a child. Antonio spoke back in surprise: "Why, brother, you ought to be happy. Have you never read James 1:2?" His logic is direct. Once someone tried to win him away from grace and get him under law. As quick as a flash Antonio replied, "Let me tell you, man, if it were not for the grace of God I would throw you into yonder corner."

A spiritist once attempted to beguile him with the theory of reincarnation. Antonio listened respectfully as an Indian should to one of the Spanish-speaking race, but all the time he prayed. When it came his turn to speak, it was with an original argument given in a quiet, assured way. "My dear sir," he said, "the Bible tells of only one reincarnation, and that was when the devil entered the serpent to tempt Eve."

As Antonio studied the Word his soul burned within him to be telling others of the Saviour's love. He witnessed as much as he could while he worked his little farm to earn his living, but he wanted to do more. His faithful qualities and knowledge of the Scriptures were made known to Mr. Bishop, a missionary in Guatemala City, who employed him as a colporteur evangelist to work under the Bible House of Los Angeles. Antonio graduated from the school in the forest on the mountainside and, like his Master, now went out to seek the lost.

To Every Creature

"From the rising of the sun unto the going down of the same the Lord's name is to be praised" (Ps. 113:3). This was the verse which Antonio Bac sent to Reverend Edward B. Dinwiddie, general secretary of the Pioneer Mission Agency, in a letter of appeal for more missionaries. It was the great desire of Antonio's heart that the saving name of Jesus be proclaimed from east to west and north to south. He knew no other ambition. He was willing to make any sacrifice and undergo any hardship in order that everyone might hear the glad tidings. He was on the trail almost constantly, but it was not a thirst for thrills or excitement which kept him going. It was the love of God constraining and the thought of lost souls impelling, the challenge of Rom. 15:20, which ever drove him on to new and harder fields.

The task of a colporteur is a hard one, and yet there is no more joyful service. It is a work which develops the courage, tact and skill of the servant of God as do few others. It more closely than any other approximates the way Jesus of Nazareth performed His evangelizing ministry. The colporteur evangelist is constantly with people. When in town he goes from house to house giving out the Word wherever he can gain a hearing. Sometimes a crowd will gather on the street and an expositional sermon will follow. Every brand of argument the devil has invented must be met at an instant's notice. The crowd must be kept in hand lest some troublemaker cause a riot. In personal work every variety of human nature is encountered. Some listen respectfully, others curse, and many are indifferent. An appropriate verse of Scripture and a special mode of approach is needed for each individual. The prayerful, persistent worker will be developed in spirituality, quick wit, and knowledge of the Bible. Many like to preach who are afraid to do personal work. They would become much better preachers if they would develop an ability for the latter. Were the writer to be in evangelical churches, he would require every aspirant to the ministry to try his hand at colporteur evangelism.

Some people take up such work readily. Others learn only after much labor. No seminary or training school will fit one fully. Persistent, prayerful practice is absolutely necessary. Antonio Bac was naturally courageous, so that he was saved the experience of many others who swallow hard with a palpitating heart while walking by a man two or three times before being able to speak to him of his soul's salvation.

Antonio had to learn patience and tenderness. It was too easy for him, at first, to impatiently tell an unrepentant listener that he was bound for hell. The school in the forest, however, had made him well acquainted with the sword of the Spirit and, full of faith, he quickly became a valuable colporteur.

As an example of the tact which he developed, let me tell the following story: One day Antonio saw a plumber working about the drainpipes of a house. He approached with a tract and asked him if he would like to read something dealing with his soul's salvation. The plumber looked up, saw that Antonio was an Indian and an *evangelista*, for no one had ever shown such interest in his soul. With great disdain he replied, "Don't bother me. I don't believe in God nor the devil nor any of that stuff." Antonio meekly sat down on a nearby stone and watched the plumber work.

Soon the man found difficulty in fitting the pipes alone. Antonio saw his chance and asked if he might help. His services were gratefully accepted. The task was difficult and the plumber showed great skill which called forth admiration from Antonio. The workman warmed up and became talkative.

Then another difficult point presented itself in the work and both became silent while the artisan deftly went about his task. When it was finished, Antonio exclaimed, "How remarkable! I don't understand it." "You don't understand what?" replied the other. "Why, how is it," said the evangelist, "that you, who are such an exceptionally intelligent man and can do your work so skillfully, can yet behold the universe which God has so wonderfully made and say that you don't believe in God?" The question struck home; the plumber dropped his tools and listened attentively to the way of salvation.

Antonio's first call was to his own people, the Indians. For their sake he was willing to put off the clothes of the Spanish race to which he had become accustomed as a soldier and put on again the woolen apron distinctive of his town. It was a hard step but a necessary one and Antonio took great joy in it, as he did in every sacrifice he felt God called him to make. He would not think of going out to evangelize without his Indian costume, for its usefulness was second only to his Bible. He reveled in his ability to slip up unawares on other Indians. He would see a group of burden-bearers resting by the roadside. Nothing could be more natural than the way Antonio sat down near them also to rest. They were not afraid of him as they would have been had he dressed in Spanish clothes. Soon a conversation began, and before they were ready to go on a whole group had been evangelized.

But while his first effort was in behalf of the Indians, he was also able upon many occasions to give the reason for the hope that was in him to those of the other race. Once he and a fellow worker were climbing a mountain grade from the hot coastal plain to the highlands of Solola. A priest passed them on horseback. Antonio respectfully handed him a tract. Further on, they saw where the priest had had his companion burn it. The trail led through an uninhabited forest. As night began to fall, they came to a hut where they would have to ask for lodging or else travel on into the night to the next habitation. But what was their surprise to find that the priest had sought shelter in the same place!

Antonio's companion wanted to go on. The intrepid worker looked at him and asked why. "Look at the priest's horse tied there," was the reply. "The priest is spending the night here and he may have the owner molest us." "I don't care," said Antonio, "you may go on if you wish but I'm going to stop here." They both entered the yard. The priest was warming himself by the fire just inside the hut. When he saw Antonio he called to him, "Hello there, Indian. What are you carrying in that bag?" "The Word of God," came the reply. "Well, bring the Word of God here and I'll put it in the fire," said the priest.

Antonio came up to the hut and in a humble but un-frightened way spoke as follows: "Oh, no, sir. This Book does not deserve the fire. You and I are the ones that de-serve to be burned for we are sinners, but this Book tells of how Christ gave His life that we might live." The priest changed tactics and offered Antonio a place by the fire, but whispered to his attendant that he should instruct the land-lady not to sell the colporteurs any food. When Antonio's companion went to buy some tortillas he was denied. He came and told Antonio who was still sitting near the priest.

In a surprised voice that could be heard throughout the hut Antonio replied, "But tell the woman that my money is just as good as his." The tortillas were secured and eaten and after everyone about the place had heard of Him who is the Bread of Life, the two workers spread their blankets upon the ground out on the open porch and went to sleep while their antagonist occupied a bed in the interior.

Upon one occasion an Indian mayor drove Antonio out of town with a shotgun. As soon as a higher official in the county seat had chastised the mayor, Antonio was right back at work in the same place. He knew no fear. A group of believers were once walking down the street when they saw a procession of images coming toward them preceded by a band and surrounded by a crowd of Indians, many of them drunk. It was a dangerous thing for a believer to pass by such a procession. He could not conscientiously remove his hat for that would be showing respect to the idols, and yet if he did not he was apt to be ill treated. When some of these believers noticed that the street was blocked with a procession they called to Antonio, who was busily con-versing with a companion a short distance ahead, and told him to come back and enter a side street with them.

Antonio asked why. He was told to look down the street.
He did so but seemed not to see the procession. The look
that came over his face seemed to say, "I don't see a lion or
anything to be afraid of. What has frightened the rest of
you?" His attitude brought courage to the other hearts
and together they walked through the crowd of idolatrous
worshipers without being bothered.

Antonio had a keen sense of humor. He once evangelized an old Indian hammock-maker. When through, he
said that he was thinking of buying a hammock. The old
man showed him one that was for sale. Antonio looked at
it and tried it, and then remarked, "This is a bad hammock." "Why?" asked the Indian. "Oh," replied the worker
with a laugh, "if I buy it, it will make me lazy."

When the cost of living was going up, the year after the
earthquake destroyed Guatemala City, Mr. Bishop decided
to raise Antonio's wages from 300 pesos to 350. When Antonio noticed the extra fifty he wanted to return them, saying that he had no desire for this world's goods. Anyone
who looked at him would have known it without being
told. He and his family all dressed in little better than rags;
their food was plain tortillas and beans, with a slight varia-
tion at times; their home was a simple hut built on rented
soil; and they owned no land of their own. But Antonio felt
that the raise was not needed and he sent it in as an offering
toward rebuilding the church in Guatemala City which had
been destroyed by earthquake.

Antonio believed in Ephesians 2:10. Early in the morning
he committed the day's work to God and believed that
every step would be for His honor and glory. One day,
when passing through a certain town on his way home, he
was taken by the officials and required to carry a heavy

load to the next town. When the writer asked why he had not objected, since he carried papers which would have exempted him from such service, he replied that he took it as an exceptional opportunity to evangelize the officials.

Once Antonio and another worker had reached Patzum ahead of me to arrange for a service. What was my surprise upon arriving at the town to find that two workers were busy carrying lime with a troop of other enforced laborers. I asked them the reason and they replied that they had been taken by the authorities and forced to help in the building of a sepulcher for a child of the military commander. I was quite put out and offered to register a complaint. Antonio said, "No, please don't. We are having a wonderful time evangelizing our fellow workers."

It was a sad day early in 1920 when the news came that Antonio Bac had been taken for military service. Talk of revolution against the tyrant who had reigned as president for twenty-two years was heard on all sides. When Antonio was placed as an artilleryman in one of the forts in the capital we wondered if we would ever see him again. Rations were scanty, pay was about three cents a day, uniforms were little more than overalls and no underwear was provided, while the men had to sleep without beds or mattresses on the cold brick floors of the barracks. Added to all this was the danger of fighting should a revolution break out. It came, and Antonio was right in the midst of it. During the preceding weeks he had been faithful in evangelizing his comrades and officers, although most of them made fun of him. His captain had been especially worldly and skeptical. But with death in sight, ideas change.

One day after a severe hour's fighting, the captain slipped back beside Antonio and said, "Tell me again,

please, all that you have said about the way of salvation."
Antonio, under shot and shell, gladly opened up to him the
Scriptures. Who knows but what Antonio's having been
taken for military service may have resulted in the salvation of that official. Antonio at least never complained of
having to go.

The revolution triumphed and Antonio was permitted to
return home. He was just an Indian and had fought only
because compelled to do so. He belonged to neither party
and was always careful not to mix in politics. Even among
the unconverted there was a saying in these countries where
"the sacred right to revolt" is often resorted to that he who
sows politics will reap the whirlwind. Antonio is even more
careful now that he is an ambassador of the King of Kings.

The writer once received a letter from Antonio, who was
discouraged. An unfaithful worker had been discharged
and was trying to dishearten the other workers. Antonio
had been pierced at a vulnerable point. He had prided himself upon having sacrificed everything to the Lord and now
this man had showed him the passage in John 10:12 and
had called him a hireling because he was receiving a salary.
For fear that it might be true, Antonio wrote that he felt as
though he would have to leave the work.

I called his attention to the fact that the hireling in the
Lord's parable had fled and left the sheep because he loved
them not, but that this could not be true of him. Then I
quoted I Cor. 9:14 and 11:8 to prove that he had a right to
a salary. Antonio, however, continued quite unhappy until
he received a letter from Mr. Bishop telling him to hunt up
new places to work where the Gospel had never been
preached. The vision came afresh. His Lord had said "to
every creature," and he would go on with this in view.

There on his knees in the forest he had at the very time of his conversion made a contract with God to give his life to Him, and he would fulfill his bargain. On and on he would go. Over mountain, valley and coastal plain, in towns, villages, plantations and out-of-the-way hamlets, he would hunt.

But there arose another problem. Someone in the States had ceased to give, and the Bible House of Los Angeles had notified that they could maintain their Indian colporteur no longer. That "man's extremity is God's opportunity" was true in this case and a new and larger field of service was opening to Antonio Bac.

"Prepared Unto Every Good Work"

Six miles from Antonio Bac's mountain home was situated the town of Acatenango. Like so many of the highland towns in Guatemala, it is made up of a mixed population of Indians and ladinos (the local name for the Spanish-speaking mixed race). The Gospel had already found an entrance among the ladino inhabitants but at the time of Antonio's conversion no Indians had yet believed, and few indeed had even heard the Gospel. Antonio soon began making his way toward town with his life-giving message.

His first attempt in that direction was shortly after believing before he had become a colporteur. He went with Bible in hand to a neighboring plantation on the road to town. He wondered how he could commence. Upon arriving, he found the planter busy overseeing his laborers as they gathered in the harvest of corn. Antonio congratulated him upon the abundance of long, yellow ears. The planter told him to look at the bins, however. "See there," he said dejectedly, "this year's crop doesn't come up halfway to the mark left on the wall by last year's storage. The bins are practically empty." As quick as a flash Antonio took advantage of his chance. "And you, sir," came his reply, "are you not afraid that you, like those bins of corn, will not come up to the mark when you appear before God in judgment?" The planter willingly listened as verses of Scripture were explained, after which he gave Antonio permission to preach to his laborers.

But to enter the town itself was far more difficult than to evangelize the surrounding farms. The Indians on the farms lost the old exclusive town spirit. While they continued to live in the town proper, they were slaves of localism. They disliked anything that looked like interference upon the part of natives of other towns. However, Antonio soon began house-to-house visitation in Acatenango.

Finally, a man by the name of Santos Chic professed to accept Christ, together with his wife and daughters. Very happy over the early harvest near home, Antonio left on one of his long colportage trips. Upon his return he found Santos wavering under the awful persecution brought to bear upon him. Antonio was able to get him back onto his feet, but a few days later had to leave again on another long trip. Santos proved to be a very weak Christian, and doubly weak when Antonio was away on trips. He quit drinking, however, and began to prosper. Soon he had paid off his debts and was able to buy a calf.

The possession of livestock by an Indian is a sign of wealth. Folks began to talk when they saw Santos' calf. Some said that he had been paid for "entering" the Gospel. Various views were given, but all agreed that Santos "had changed religions for the money that was in it." The bitter, contemptuous charges drove the poor man frantic. Angered beyond measure, he returned to rum in an attempt to drown his wrath. The neighbors rejoiced to see him drunk once more and the saloonkeepers gave him all his thirst demanded, looking upon the newly-bought calf as security.

When Antonio returned again to visit Acatenango he found the fruit of his previous labors destroyed. Santos was ashamed, but he refused to have anything more to do with the Gospel.

But Antonio had sowed the good seed in other soil as well. Upon the Chicasan grade on the road to Itzapa he had once met an Acatenango Indian by the name of Francisco Canu. Francisco did not know how to read, but he gladly received a gospel of John, since Antonio assured him that it was the Word of God and he had a friend who could read it to him. A few days later as he was working in his cornfield, he became tired and stopped for a smoke. His cigars, however, had become broken by careless handling. What should he do? As he felt in his pockets, he came upon the gospel of John. He tore out a leaf, carefully rolled in it his broken cigar, and had his smoke.

This he repeated for several days until he noticed that only a few pages remained in the Book. Then his conscience began to hurt him. He was burning up the Word of God and had not even made an effort to find out what it said! There was no more smoking of broken cigars in that fashion for Francisco. He looked up his friend, and together they pondered over the remaining pages of the Gospel until they became convinced of the truth of its message.

Just at that time special services were being held in Acatenango. Antonio was busier than ever. A young Indian came to the door one evening. Antonio invited him in and, after the service, received the youth's profession of faith. This young man took Antonio to the home of the Canu family, and as a result, both Francisco and his father accepted Christ. At the same time, Santos came back to the

Lord. God had formed an Indian congregation in Acate-nango. As a place of meeting, Francisco gladly gave a brand-new hut which he had just built to become an official image deposit. Antonio undertook to pastor the little flock but this was very difficult while he continued to work as a colporteur, for he was away so much that he could rarely visit his charge more than once a month. The result was that the little flock was left largely in the hands of the ladino elders and workers for shepherding.

Now, no matter how humble a ladino may be, he invari-ably considers himself as being far above an Indian. Most ladino believers, when trying to work with Indian con-verts, find it very hard to carry out the apostolic injunction not to act as "lords over God's heritage. " One of the ladino elders in Acatenango who was very solicitous about the welfare of the Indian believers caused Antonio special diffi-culty. His wife manifested the typical attitude of ladino towards Indian. The writer was once painfully hurt when he saw this woman refuse to give her hand in greeting to Antonio Bac's humble wife, merely because she was an Indian.

Antonio had learned patience, and realized that the la-dinos were anxious to help and that their many blunders were due only to old ideas of race superiority and failure to understand Indian ways. The new believers, however, were not so patient, and when Antonio was away on trips would become greatly disheartened at the unwise methods of their ladino brethren. Several times the Indian believers were at the point of turning back when Antonio or some other Indian worker would pay them a timely visit and build them up once more in the faith.

It was at this point that Antonio was released from

colportage work. One of the blessings in disguise was the fact that he could now have more time for pastoring the little congregation God had raised up under his ministry. Funds were available from another source and Antonio was employed as a pastor-evangelist. There would have been plenty for him to do in Acatenango and nearby towns, but the old thirst of Rom. 15:20 was so strong in Antonio that he could not bring himself to stand by the local field for more than half the time. But that was sufficient for a man of his makeup to accomplish a great deal.

One of his first moves forward was to begin taking up a weekly offering. A number of ladinos were present when the announcement was made. A ladino elder sprang to his feet with an energetic protest. "No," he said, "we should never take up collections. It will keep people away from our meetings. There is no need of it. I am willing to pay for the lights in our ladino chapel and you Indian elders ought to be willing to foot your own bills without asking everyone to contribute."

Antonio was calm and firm, His appeal was direct to the Scriptures. Had the elder never read I Cor. 16:1,2? There were needs for funds other than just the lights, and the Indians at least would be given their biblical privilege to contribute. The Indians came forward and gave, after which the abashed ladinos followed suit.

Francisco Canu was entrusted with the funds. An Indian believer who knew how to read would keep account of them. Soon more than 200 pesos had been gathered into the strongbox. Then the ladino elder made a discourse on Judas and how he carried the bag and pilfered from it. Others said that the amount was too large to be left with an ignorant Indian. Pressure was brought to bear upon

Francisco and Antonio, and finally the funds were turned over to a ladino treasurer. This greatly weakened the Indians' spirit of giving and Antonio carried the matter to the Indian missionary, who decided that the Indians might have a collection box of their own.

Antonio was too wise now to make a public announcement, but in a quiet way the regular Sunday offering was continued. The ladinos then decided that they had done wrong and the elder was commissioned to return the funds to the Indians. Antonio was away, but Francisco with perfect Indian logic was prepared for the occasion. "Remember," he said to the ladino elder, "your sermon on Judas. Don't forget, too, how when he came to return the thirty pieces of silver they could not be put back into the treasury." The Indians would not take the money, and so as a compromise it was invested in benches for the two chapels.

Antonio from the very start did his best to interest his little flock in missionary work. About three miles from Acatenango was a plantation. Here Antonio had been well received by both owner and men. Services were well attended and there was a promise of a large congregation. The women, however, were afraid to go to the services. Antonio appealed to his faithful helpmeet who had ever been a constant source of encouragement to him. She volunteered to take her daughter, who could sing quite well, and trudge along the nine miles from their mountain home to assist in a service at the plantation. This was done, and as a result of the house-to-house visitation work of Antonio's wife and daughter many women came out to the service that evening. It was a happy trio that returned home the next day, confident that the Lord was going to do great things in the plantation.

But clever is the hinderer! In how many ways does he go about snatching up the seed! A few days later, Antonio saw a large group of prospective believers from the plantation making their way up the trail toward his home. They carried baskets of food and the worker's heart rejoiced as he thought that they had come all that way to spend a day in studying with him the Word. Mats were spread on the floor and covered with the sumptuous meal the Indians had brought. They had spent even to the extent of buying real bread and sweets.

After the feast, Antonio prepared to start a service. One of the visitors, however, detained him, saying that they had come on a special mission. After a formal speech he asked for the hand of Antonio's daughter in marriage to a young man in the party. The old-time fire flashed in the father's eyes. Sudden proposals were nothing unusual among Indians. Even among believers a widow has been asked to marry a week after her husband's death. But what angered Antonio in this particular case was the attempt to mix worship and courtship. He administered a stern rebuke to the spokesman, but then, remembering that he was but a recent hearer of the Word, eased off with a suggestion that the couple be permitted to decide for themselves. The service was then held after which the disappointed group returned home.

There are now several little groups of believers around Acatenango. The story of the entrance of the Gospel into the village of San Diego is especially interesting as a modern miracle. Antonio had finally been able to secure a little plot of ground in Acatenango proper, and had moved to town. In San Diego lived two Indian couples who were terrible drunkards. Both men and women would get drunk Sunday after Sunday. Finally, they heard of the Gospel's power to save drunkards, and of the preacher, Antonio Bac. They decided to seek him out and make inquiries. Fearful of their neighbors, like Nicodemus of old, they went on their errand by night. They reached Acatenango early in the morning and asked where Antonio lived. Some unbelievers said that he didn't live in Acatenango but in the next town of Nejapa. In Nejapa, the seekers were told by the town officials that Antonio was an *evangelista* and such a bad man that they had made him live way off in the mountains all by himself.

Very much disheartened, the two couples returned to Acatenango and asked again for Antonio. This time they were fortunate in finding a believer who directed them to the chapel where Antonio had just begun a service. They listened attentively and at the close accepted Christ. Their changed lives were noticed by all on the plantation, but the new believers said nothing and would leave for services early Sunday morning before anyone would notice where they were going. Finally, their secret was discovered, and a mob of laborers carried them before the owner to see what he would do with them. The owner asked what was up. When they explained, he manifested real pleasure and told the mob that he wished all would accept the Gospel and so quit drinking. A neighboring planter tried to dissuade him, saying that should his laborers come to believe, they would be reformed, quickly pay off their debts and leave him. He remained firm in his first decision, however, and invited Antonio to visit the plantation regularly.

With a chapel, pastor and organization of its own, the Indian congregation in Acatenango prospered. The ladinos continued to bother, however, in a well-meaning, unwise way. They insisted upon doing the preaching even in the Indian chapel when Antonio was absent, and often when he was present, a ladino would give an hour and a half's sermon in Spanish and then offer Antonio the remaining time.

At a conference held in Acatenango, the Indians presented their plea. They wanted regular services in Cakchiquel, and they wanted them badly! They said that they were not growing in the knowledge of the Word because they could not understand Spanish well enough. They insisted upon having their own order of worship. The ladinos objected at first, but as the Spirit had time to work they saw the wisdom of the demand and conceded, so that the Indian congregation governed its own affairs and heard the Word expounded regularly in its own language. Some of the ladinos who understood Cakchiquel preferred the Indian services to their own, for they profited from Antonio's preaching.

In the summer of 1921, Frank and Herbert Toms, missionaries in Huehuetenango, opened a summer Bible school. Five Cakchiquel workers were able to attend, Trinidad Bac being among their number. Antonio longed to go but could not, for he had to keep active as a colporteur. He felt badly about it but said that God might open up such an opportunity for him later on, and, if not, that he would go ahead with his Bible and the Holy Spirit to teach him. For many months prayer had been going up to God for an Indian workers' training school. Workers had been called in monthly for a few days' study in the writer's home. But it was not sufficient, and a plan was devised to establish a school which would be in session every other month. This

would give the men, unused to study as they were, an opportunity to digest and put in practice one month that
which they had learned the previous one. It also provided
for a thorough working of the field every other month.

Reverend W. E. Robinson, a missionary in the Depart-
ment of Solola, promised to help, and his desire that the
school be located in Panajachel on the shores of Lake Atitlan was adhered to. Then came Mr. Robinson's lamented
death and the plan was delayed for several months.

In February of 1923, Mr. A. E. Anderson arrived on the
field, appointed to Indian work. Gifted of God for teaching, he became enthusiastic at once over the training
school, and at the request of his fellow missionaries agreed
to give half his time to it. School opened in March of 1923,
with Mr. Anderson and the writer serving as faculty and
four eager Indian workers as students.

Antonio Bac was among the number. At first, things
seemed strange to him. He found that he had to throw
many of his old ideas overboard. It hurt him to find that he
knew so little. The old Antonio wanted to get angry and
quit; but II Tim. 2:15 was in his Bible, and after a struggle
the humility of the Spirit won out and Antonio kept on
studying. After that he learned rapidly. How happy he was
to return to his congregation with new lessons! No wonder
the ladinos were anxious to come and hear him teach.
Other workers heard of the school and decided to attend.
Soon the number of students passed one score.

Over weekends, the students went out among the nearby
Indian towns. More than a dozen villages were found
around the shores of beautiful Lake Atitlan, and a new
ministry opened up for Antonio. Every town heard his
message of salvation. He, like his Master, found men

fishing on the lake shore and set out his net for them.

One day in Atitlan, center of the Zutujil tribe, Antonio saw an old man standing on the beach with hook and line, waiting for a bite. Antonio greeted him cordially, only to hear the gruff reply: "Who are you looking for?" "I am looking for you," answered the worker. "Do you know me?" asked the old man. "Yes," said Antonio. "Who am I?" came the puzzled retort. "You are a sinner," replied Antonio as he opened his Bible. The old man dropped his fishing pole and went to Antonio's side. "You have something I don't know anything about. Tell it to me," he appealed.

The old man was a witch doctor, a Priest of the Sun. He became greatly interested in the Gospel.

To be "prepared unto every good work" is the great ambition of Antonio Bac. To this end, he desired a barber's outfit that men might seek him. A friend in the States soon sent him one. Now he carries his kit of tools as well as the Bible. Someone is sure to ask, "Don't you clip hair?" This is the opportunity Antonio has been looking for, and soon he is found in the yard of some Indian home, clipping hair almost free of charge while explaining the Way of Life to a group of seekers after barber bargains. In this way he clips and shaves many a soul into the kingdom of God.

A short time ago Antonio was preparing to leave Acatenango for the school session in Panajachel. He had secured no one to supply his pulpit the Sundays that he would be absent. A capable believer from Patzum put in his appearance at the last service before Antonio's departure. Antonio wanted to announce that this man would hold services the next Sunday but he was afraid of a flat refusal. He merely announced a service without saying who would preach. After the meeting, he invited the Patzum believer to visit him in the morning. "I can't do it," replied the man. "You know that I have to start to work in my cornfield very early. You know it will go to ruin if I don't care for it."

"Yes," said Antonio, as he rubbed his hand through his hair with a significant smile, "and it looks to me as though something else were going to ruin." The believer caught the hint and laughed. "All right," he said, "I'll be around in the morning if you will give me a haircut bright and early."

"Any time after five o'clock," said the pastor. "Remember that it must be light enough to see, or I'll do a poor job."

Lured by the thought of a free haircut, the unsuspecting visitor delayed his start for work the next morning and went to call on Antonio. The latter had no more than seated him in the chair when he grabbed with no little force a handful of hair and with a mock-menacing voice said, "Now promise you will preach for me twice next Sunday!" Antonio's trickery worked; he extracted from the visiting brother the promise to preach.

Oh, that Antonio could seize by the locks many more Christians caught in the whirl of life's activities until they obeyed the Lord's command! Would that some giant hand could awaken all to behold the open door and enter where multitudes cry out for knowledge of the Word of God!

Antonio beckons workers to the Cakchiquels and to the other Indians of Latin America, for he yearns to extend a saving hand to other Indians from the Rio Grande to Tierra del Fuego. Come! Pray! Send! Awaken! It is your Lord's command—hasten to complete the unfinished task!

IV

William Cameron Townsend on Location in Guatemala 1917-1931: A Pictorial Documentary of a Pioneer Translator

Having completed his junior year at Occidental College of Los Angeles, W. Cameron Townsend sailed in 1917 for Guatemala to sell Spanish Bibles under appointment of the Bible House of Los Angeles, earning his passage by loading crates of fruit at the dock in San Francisco, his point of embarkation.

First of a series of quakes
rocked Guatemala City
December 25, 1917. Townsend,
asleep on the second floor of a
mission building when the first
shock came, was awakened by
his companion Elbert Robinson.
On the street later he reported,
"The earth seemed to rise right
up and hang there quivering;
walls swayed back and forth
until they could stand it no
longer, and fell. Then the earth
began to roll like the sea. We
wondered if the ground would
not open up. The city's prison
walls, two and a half feet thick,
had fallen."

Before resuming their own
Bible-selling program
Townsend and Robinson spent
several weeks aiding
missionaries in rescue and
rehabilitation efforts.

In 1919 Townsend married Elvira Malmstrom,
missionary from Chicago whom he met in
Guatemala. Together they pioneered in a
"cornstalk" home and undertook translation of
the Cakchiquel New Testament, a task they
completed in 1929. The Testament was
published by American Bible Society in 1931.

At times the Townsends wore the hand-loomed garments of the village, a practice highly approved by their Cakchiquel neighbors.

[Above] In a typical Cakchiquel Indian home, Cameron Townsend (left) introduces a foreign visitor to his friends.

[Right] A Cakchiquel evangelist and his wife prepare to travel to a neighboring village to share the "Good News."

[Above] Felix Hernandez (right), who served as printer in pioneer phases of Cakchiquel publications, appears with his family in their village, San Antonio Aguas Calientes.

[Below] In its tentative form, a page of the gospel of John in Cakchiquel (first New Testament book to be published for this Indian group).

2 La pronunciación de las letras es más bien aproximada a la pronunciación española.
3 Se han usado las nuevas letras siguientes:
(a) La ch' es ch española pronunciada con explosión.
(b) La tz se pronuncia como tz con más explosión.
(c) La k' representa el primer sonido de la palabra k'ij (sol) o (día).
(d) La g' se pronuncia como k mientras uno está pensando g gutural. Se encuentra en palabras como g'o (hay) eig'uin (conmigo)
4 La x se pronuncia como sh inglesa así como se ha acostumbrado en las lenguas indígenas de Guatemala.
5 Esta obra está en la forma de Cakchiquel usada en San Juan Comalapa pero será fácil adoptarla a muchos otros pueblos haciendo las variaciones necesarias mientras se lee.

Imprenta Cakchiquel
"Woodsum"
San Antonio A. C., Guatemala
1923

...on, y rija ri sek quichin ri achiha.
5 Y ri sek dusakirisaj rupan ri k'akun y ri k'okun man xk'ax ta rija chiquiv ec h.
6 G'o jun achin rutakompe Dios, rubinihan Juan.
7 Jare xpe achehel chin conojel tiquinimaj roma rija.
8 Man rija ta ri sek, xachuvahic ri sek.
9 Jari jun sek kitsij ja guerusakirisaj conojel ri achiha, dipe chuva ch'ulef.
10 G'ovi chuya ch'ulef, y rija xbanun; y ri ruva chulef man xquetamaj ta ruvech.
11 Quig'uin richin xpevi, y rije man xquig'ben ta ruvech.
12 Mas conojel ri xeg'amon ruvech, xuya quik'ij chin xeoc ralg'ual Dios, ri achique gueniman pa rubi.
13 Rije man ta chi quig', ni ru tihij, ni ru achin, mas richin Dios.
14 Ri Verbo xupori tihij xg'oje chi y xkatget ru gloria ri juney ru G'ajol ri Tatahixel, nojnek rig'uin lo-

1920 marked the beginning of a new chapter in pioneer missions when L.L. Legters, invited by Townsend, visited the Cakchiquel field. Witnessing an emerging indigenous church, he realized the potential of reaching all the Bibleless languages of the world. The Townsend-Legters vision became a reality in the founding of Summer Institute of Linguistics in 1934, and later (1942) Wycliffe Bible Translators.

Cameron and Elvira Townsend (in Cakchiquel dress, far left) invited the first Cakchiquel believers to participate in a Bible conference in 1920. L.L. Legters (far right) spoke through an interpreter to the Indian believers.

Legters, with Elvira and Cameron Townsend (center rear), inspired Cakchiquel leaders to evangelize their own people as the New Testament was being translated.

In the village of Panajachel on Lake Atitlan, the Townsends served under the Central American Mission while completing translation of the Cakchiquel New Testament.

The "cornstalk" house of early days was soon replaced by a wooden bungalow on the lake, a home where Indian visitors were always welcome.

Many Cakchiquel villages, nestled around the scenic lake and terraced on volcanic slopes, were evangelized by Cakchiquel workers trained in Panajachel. The lake ministry was "launched" by Townsend and workers he trained.

In 1922 Townsend's co-worker W.E. Robinson drowned in Lake Atitlan. To honor his pioneer work among the Cakchiquels a training school for Indian workers, Robinson Bible Institute, was established in Panajachel.

Mr. A. E. Bishop (far left) of the Central American Mission with Elvira and Cameron Townsend and students of the Institute.

First graduation exercises of Robinson Bible Institute.

[Above] The advent of the auto was an asset to pioneer work—with built-in risks. A natural handyman, Townsend became proficient in auto mechanics, including extensive roadside repair.

[Below] Once considered creations of Satan, autos later became symbols of prestige among the village boys. Cakchiquel youths dreamed of driving the once-dreaded mechanical beasts.

[Above] Cameron's brother Paul Townsend (1) and Consul General Holland (2) leave Panajachel for a trip through isolated Cakchiquel villages. Also shown: Holland's son and Elvira Townsend.

[Left] W. F. Jordan of American Bible Society traveled trails of Guatemala with Townsend for a firsthand look at the people for whom the Bible was being translated. In his book Central American Indians and the Bible he described his ventures, providing personal insights into Townsend's early dreams for work beyond Cakchiquel borders.

Wherever Townsend worked, his dream of Indian education became a reality. He built schools, shops, hospitals—and trained Indians to serve as instructors and administrators.

[Above] The Louise Heim Home for Indian children provided love, care, and training for underprivileged Indian children.

[Below] Mechanical training for Indian boys prepared them to take their place beside "ladinos" in the inevitable industrialization of Guatemala.

Two young residents of the Louise Heim Home.

The dream still lives, and grows. Now offering a four-year curriculum, Robinson Bible Institute continues under the aegis of the Central American Mission. [Above] Students of the modern Robinson Bible Institute enjoy a noon meal.

A copy of the newly-published Cakchiquel New Testament was presented to President of Guatemala General Ubico on May 19, 1931. Trinidad Bac, co-translator of the Testament, and R.R. Gregory of American Bible Society accompanied Townsend at the historic presentation ceremony in the presidential palace in Guatemala City.

[Above] Fifty years after Townsend's arrival in the land of the Cakchiquels he is honored by many there who still remember his pioneer Indian work.

[Below] An Indian woman recalls early days when believers were few; her friend Townsend remembers, too.

*Townsend with neighboring Tzutujil tribesmen,
Mayan-language cousins of the Cakchiquels.*

Once a teacher, always a teacher: Townsend reads the New Testament to a Cakchiquel lad in San Antonio Aguas Calientes, the village in which he pioneered 50 years earlier.

A Word from W. Cameron Townsend, 1981

"Oh, Mr. President, this book you handed me is in my language and it tells about God! Where can I get one?"

A Cakchiquel Indian was speaking. He had been sent by his village to ask the president of Guatemala to give an order that evangelicals should not live in their town. The Cakchiquels wanted to continue in their age-old witchcraft, superstitions, and drunken festivals. Early in the year, however, the president had been presented the first New Testament in Cakchiquel (May, 1931). He had thanked the translators (Trinidad Bac, Joe Chicol, and W. C. Townsend) and also the publishers (American Bible Society) and then had put it on a shelf in his office. Now he used it to open the eyes of the man whose village had sent him to oppose evangelicals. The eventual result was a new man freed by the Word in his own tongue.

The Word of God in every tongue is the goal of the Summer Institute of Linguistics, from the scientific viewpoint. The grammar alone is a tremendous task. To learn and analyze an unwritten language takes several years. Then comes the tedious task of producing a good translation. This, however, results in transformed lives.

Will you volunteer? Between two and three thousand local language groups scattered in many lands are still waiting. Fifty years have elapsed since President Ubico of Guatemala used the first Cakchiquel New Testament so wisely. The Summer Institute of Linguistics, organized in 1936, and Wycliffe Bible Translators, organized six years later, have given or are in the process of giving the Word for the first time to some 800 language groups in thirty lands. The present team of 4,000 translators and support personnel must be more than doubled in order to reach 2,000 more tongues. Will you help?

Chet Bitterman wanted to translate the Word for a tribe, but like Stephen, God had other plans for him. Will you be one to pick up the task he was forced to lay down? "Pray ye the Lord of the harvest that he will send forth laborers into his harvest." And don't be surprised if He sends *you*, yourself, as He did His disciples whom He had first ordered to pray (Matt. 9:38 and 10:5).